Anonymous

**The Erie route**

Anonymous

**The Erie route**

ISBN/EAN: 9783337145477

Printed in Europe, USA, Canada, Australia, Japan

Cover: Foto ©Andreas Hilbeck / pixelio.de

More available books at **www.hansebooks.com**

# THE ERIE ROUTE:

## A GUIDE OF THE

# NEW YORK, LAKE ERIE & WESTERN RAILWAY

## AND ITS BRANCHES,

WITH

SKETCHES OF THE CITIES, VILLAGES, SCENERY AND OBJECTS
OF INTEREST ALONG THE ROUTE,

AND

RAILROAD, STEAMBOAT AND STAGE CONNECTIONS.

REVISED BY

P. L. TUCKER,

*Of the General Passenger Department of the New York, Lake Erie
& Western Railroad.*

MAP AND ILLUSTRATIONS

Copyright, 1887, by
TAINTOR BROTHERS & CO.

NEW YORK:
TAINTOR BROTHERS & CO.
18 AND 20 ASTOR PLACE.

## INDEX.

| | PAGE | | PAGE |
|---|---|---|---|
| Jamestown | 48? | Point Chautauqua | 48b |
| Jersey City | 17 | Port Jervis | 25 |
| Kanona | 64 | Port Jervis and Monticello R. R. | 78 |
| Kirkwood | 31 | Ramapo | 21 |
| Lackawaxen | 27 | Ramsey's | 20 |
| Lake View | 18 | Rathboneville | 42 |
| Lancaster | 53 | Red Creek | 67 |
| Lakewood | 48b | Ridgewood | 19 |
| Leroy | 70 | Rochester | 67 |
| Liberty | 63 | Rochester Division | 62 |
| Linden | 52 | Route of St. Lawrence River | 86 |
| Little Valley | 47 | Rutherford Park | 17 |
| Livonia | 65 | Rush | 66 |
| Lordville | 29 | Salamanca | 47 |
| Lorillard's | 21 | Savona | 62 |
| Mahwah | 20 | Scio | 44 |
| Mayville | 48a | Scottsville | 67 |
| Middletown | 24 | Shohola | 27 |
| Minor Branches of the Erie | 72 | Short Cut to Newburgh | 75 |
| Monroe | 22 | Sloatsburg | 21 |
| Montgomery | 78 | Smithboro | 36 |
| Montgomery and Wallkill Valley Branch | 78 | Smith's Mills | 48 |
| | | Southfields | 21 |
| Monticello | 78 | South Livonia | 65 |
| Mt. Morris | 84 | Southport | 38 |
| Narrowsburg | 28 | Springwater | 65 |
| Newark | 72 | Stafford | 71 |
| Newburgh | 76 | Stockport | 29 |
| Newburgh (Short-Cut) Branch | 75 | Suffern | 20 |
| New Windsor | 75 | Summit | 29 |
| New York, Pennsylvania and Ohio R. R. | 82 | Susquehanna | 31 |
| | | Suspension Bridge | 61 |
| Niagara Falls | 59 | Swainville | 49 |
| Niagara Falls Branch | 57 | Tappan | 74 |
| Northern R. R. of New Jersey | 73 | Tioga Center | 36 |
| Nunda | 50 | Tonawanda | 58 |
| Nyack | 74 | Town Line | 33 |
| Olean | 46 | Turner's | 22 |
| Otisville | 25 | Union | 33 |
| Owego | 33 | Vandalia | 46 |
| Oxford | 22 | Wallkill Valley Branch | 78 |
| Painted Post | 41 | Wallace's | 64 |
| Passaic | 18 | Warsaw | 52 |
| Paterson | 18 | Warwick | 76 |
| Paterson and Newark Branch | 72 | Warwick Branch | 76 |
| Perrysburg | 48 | Watkins Glen | 39 |
| Phillipsville | 44 | Waverly | 37 |
| Piermont | 20 | Wayland | 64 |
| Pine Grove | 28 | Webster | 65 |
| Pine Island | 77 | Wellsburg....37 Wellsville | 44 |
| Pine Island Branch | 77 | West Junction | 40 |
| Pond Eddy | 26 | White Mills | 79 |
| Portage | 50 | Woodside | 73 |

# THE AMERICAN,

## BOSTON.

CENTRAL LOCATION.     PERFECT VENTILATION.

### UNEXCEPTIONABLE TABLE.

PARTICULARLY DESIRABLE

### FOR FAMILIES AND SUMMER TOURISTS.

SIX STAIRWAYS FROM TOP TO BOTTOM.

With every security against fire.

| | | |
|---|---|---|
| Rooms with Meals, | $3.00 **PER DAY** and upwards. | According to Size and Location. |
| Rooms only. | $1.00 **PER DAY** and upwards. | |

### THE NEAREST FIRST CLASS HOTEL

TO NORTHERN AND EASTERN DEPOTS,

"It is one of the most attractive and best managed of New England Hotels."—*N. Y. Mail.*

**HENRY B. RICE & CO.**     near *Hanover, Washington St.*

**The Full Principal Sum** will be paid in case of loss of both feet, both hands, a hand and a foot, or the entire sight of both eyes, by accident.

**ACCIDENTS** are always happening to those who "DON'T TRAVEL MUCH" as well as to those who do. The quietest

**PROFESSIONAL ✢ AND ✢ BUSINESS ✢ MEN**

are as liable as any others to the thousand hazards of life, at home or abroad.

"MORAL: INSURE IN THE TRAVELERS."

**THE TRAVELERS INSURANCE COMPANY, HARTFORD, CONN.**

Original **ACCIDENT COMPANY** OF AMERICA, LARGEST IN THE WORLD; Also, Best of Life Companies.

ISSUES

**ACCIDENT POLICIES,** covering injuries received in Travel, Work, or Sport.
**BEST LIFE POLICY** in the Market. Indefeasible, Non-Forfeitable, World-Wide.

PAID POLICY-HOLDERS $13,500,000.

*All Claims paid without Discount, and immediately on receipt of Satisfactory Proofs.*

Assets, **$9,111,000.** Surplus, **$2,129,000.**

J. G. BATTERSON, Pres.          RODNEY DENNIS, Sec.

**One-third the Principal Sum** will be paid for loss of a single hand or foot.

# THE ERIE RAILWAY.

THE NEW YORK, LAKE ERIE, AND WESTERN RAILROAD, known the world over as the Erie Railway, may be said to have been the pioneer in the great system of American trunk lines. At the time it was constructed it was the most stupendous engineering feat ever attempted in this country. Railroad building was in its infancy when the engineers made their report on the feasibility of the enterprise. After a survey of the route proposed for the road, they declared it was impracticable, because of certain grades which it would be impossible for a locomotive to overcome; so meagre was the knowledge of the possibilities of a railroad science at that day. There were several local railroads in the country, but, beyond the fact that they had demonstrated the practicability and importance of iron rails and steam motive power as a means of transportation, and awakened an interest in the matter among men of enterprise and progressive ideas, they had done nothing towards making an application of the new system to the wants of the country at large. The idea of a highway of iron rails from the ocean to the shores of Lake Erie was therefore received by the country as a proposition of madmen. People had stood aghast, also, when the far-seeing Maurice Wurts came forward with his project for a canal that would connect the anthracite coal regions of Northern Pennsylvania with the city of New York, years before there was a mile of railroad track in America. But he carried his project to successful completion, and his success strengthened the faith of the fathers of the Erie in the feasibility of their grand scheme. Projected in 1835, the New York and Erie Railroad was constructed by piecemeal. Such barriers as jealousy and persistent opposition could prompt, and a scant treasury but feebly contend against, were thrown in the way of the enterprise for nearly twenty years, and it was not until 1852 that a line of

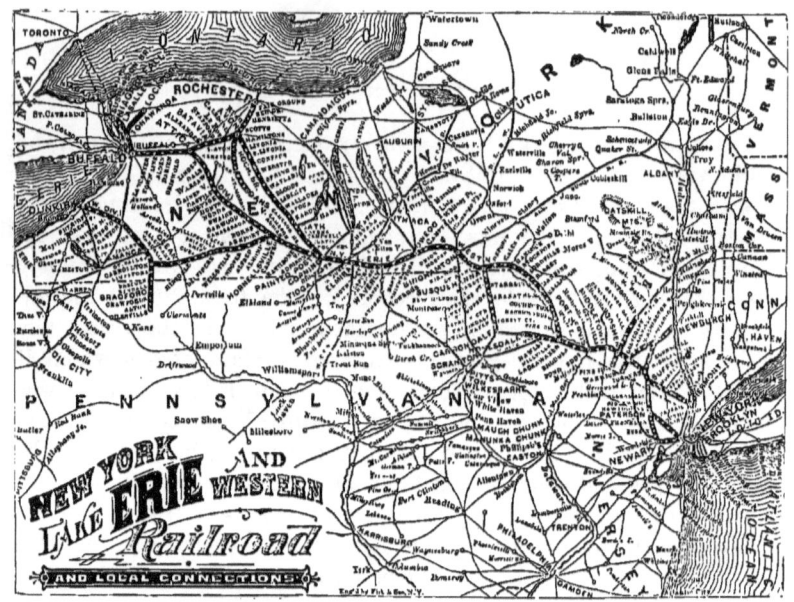

## ERIE RAILWAY ROUTE.

rails between the Hudson River and Lake Erie gave easy and quick thoroughfare for the trade and travel of the East and West. Gradually the pioneer of American trunk lines gathered strength and power, in spite of the abuse and spoliation that corrupt managements and designing men subjected it to. No grander struggle ever was known in the history of financial or commercial relations than that which this famous railroad made for its corporate existence during the *long years of its bondage.* Delivered at last, the New York, Lake Erie and Western stands to-day a giant among the railroads of America. The single track of cast-iron rails that less than a quarter of a century ago led trains, few and far between, across the Empire State, has given place to a double track of the finest steel. The interests of the road are no longer local. Beside being our immediate thoroughfare, the Erie Company now has entire control of the New York, Pennsylvania and Ohio Railroad, under lease effected in 1883, and the new Chicago and Atlantic Railway, which was constructed in the sole interest of the Erie. The influence of the Erie system has come to be a power from the Atlantic to the Pacific in this country, as well as in commercial and financial circles across the sea.

The road originally began at Piermont, on the Hudson River, twenty-five miles above New York city; but in 1853 arrangements were made by which the roads of other companies, extending from Suffern, in New York, to Jersey City, were leased in perpetuity to the Erie Company, and with the completion of the tunnel through Bergen Hill a few years later, steamboat transportation to and from Piermont was avoided. The trains now run directly to Jersey City, opposite New York, where the company has erected spacious freight and passenger depots, and established a line of ferries which convey the passenger either to Chambers street, or Twenty-third street, New York city, and connect with Annex boats for Brooklyn.

### ITINERARY OF THE ERIE RAILWAY.

The grand trunk of the road extends from Jersey City to Dunkirk, on the shores of Lake Erie; but from Corning, a division extends to Rochester, and another from Hornellsville to Buffalo. With these and its numerous branches, the New York, Lake Erie and Western Railway proper comprises 1,037 miles of track. The lease of the New York, Pennsylvania and Ohio Railroad gives it control of 496 miles

## ERIE RAILWAY ROUTE.

of track, and the completion of the Chicago and Atlantic Railway adds 269 miles to the Erie system. The Erie Railway also controls and operates the New York and Greenwood Lake Railway, extending from Jersey City to Greenwood Lake, N. Y., and by branch to Orange, N. J., 47 miles in all ; the Northern Railroad of New Jersey, from Jersey City to Nyack, 29 miles ; the Bradford, Eldred and Cuba Railroad, from Wellsville to Eldred, 33 miles, and from Bolivar to Cuba, 21 miles; the Bradford, Bordell and Kinzua Railroad, from Bradford to Eldred, 23½ miles, and from Kinzua Junction to Smethport, 16 miles; the Tonawanda Valley Railroad from Cuba to Attica, 59 miles.

These roads are an important division of the narrow gauge system in the Pennsylvania oil, coal and lumber regions and the new salt fields of western New York. Recently the Bradford Branch of the Erie has been extended to Johnsonburg, Pa., a distance of 53 miles. It is on this extension that the highest railroad bridge in the world had to be constructed, across Kinzua Gorge, the height of the structure being 303 feet. These various acquisitions to the Erie System make a grand total of track now operated by the Erie of 2,030½ miles.

The Erie Railway is separated into seven grand Divisions—the Eastern, Delaware, Susquehanna, Rochester, Buffalo, Western, and Buffalo and Southwestern, as follows :

### EASTERN DIVISION.

Jersey City to Port Jervis, 88 miles. E. O. Hill, Supt , Jersey City.

Branches.—Newark Branch—Jersey City to Paterson, 17 miles. Piermont Branch—Suffern to Piermont, 18 miles. Newburgh Short Cut—Turner's to Newburgh, 16 miles. Newburgh Branch—Greycourt to Newburgh, 16 miles. Pine Island Branch—Goshen to Pine Island, 11¾ miles. Montgomery Branch—Goshen to Montgomery, 10 miles. Crawford Branch—Middletown to Pine Bush, 13 miles. Total miles of track, 189.

### DELAWARE DIVISION.

Port Jervis to Susquehanna, 105 miles. Edgar Van Allen, Supt., Port Jervis.

Branches—Honesdale Branch—Lackawaxen to Honesdale, 25 miles. Jefferson Branch—Susquehanna to Carbondale, 38 miles. Erie and Wyoming Valley—Hawley to Pittston, 42 miles. Total miles of track, 210.

### SUSQUEHANNA DIVISION.

Susquehanna to Hornellsville, 139 miles. R. B. Cable, Superintendent, Elmira, N. Y. Tioga, R. R.—Elmira to Hoytville, 61 miles. Total miles of track, 200.

# ERIE RAILWAY ROUTE.

### ROCHESTER DIVISION.

Corning to Rochester, 94 miles. W. J. Murphy, Supt., Buffalo, N Y.

Branches.—Attica Branch—Avon to Attica, 34 miles. Dansville and Mount Morris Branch—Avon to Dansville, 30 miles. Total miles of track, 158.

### BUFFALO DIVISION.

Hornellsville to Buffalo, 91 miles. W. J. Murphy, Supt., Buffalo.

Branches—Lockport Branch—Tonawanda to Lockport, 14 miles. Niagara Falls Branch—Buffalo to Niagara Falls and Suspension Bridge, 23 miles. Erie and International R. R. Total miles of track, 127.

### WESTERN DIVISION.

Hornellsville to Dunkirk, 128 miles. W. B. Coffin, Superintendent, Hornellsville.

Branches.—Bradford Branch—Carrollton to Johnsonburg, 53 miles. Toby Branch, 12 miles. Total miles of track, 193.

### BUFFALO AND SOUTHWESTERN DIVISION.

Buffalo to Jamestown, 68 miles. C. A. Brunn, Superintendent, Buffalo. Total miles of track, 68.

Total miles operated by Erie Railway proper, 1,037.

### LOCAL LINES OPERATED BY THE ERIE RAILWAY.

New York and Greenwood Lake Railroad.—Jersey City to Greenwood Lake, 43 miles. Hon. A. S. Hewitt, President, New York; John N. Abbott, General Passenger Agent, New York; Stephen Smith, Superintendent, Jersey City.

Northern Railroad of New Jersey.—Jersey City to Nyack, N. Y., 29 miles. O. A. Roorback, Superintendent; John N. Abbott, General Passenger Agent, New York.

### LOCAL CONNECTIONS OF THE ERIE RAILWAY.

At Montgomery, N. Y. (*via* Montgomery Branch from Goshen), with the Wallkill Valley Railroad for Kingston and all points in the Catskill Mts., *via* Ulster and Delaware Railroad from Kingston.

At Greycourt, N. Y., with the Warwick Valley Railroad for Warwick, N. Y., Franklin, N. J., and Easton, Pa., and points in Pennsylvania Coal Regions *via* Sussex Railroad and from Franklin.

At Newburgh, N. Y., with the New York and New England Railroad for Boston, Hartford, and all principal New England points.

## ERIE RAILWAY ROUTE.

At Middletown, N. Y., with the New York, Ontario, and Western Railroad for Ellenville, Delhi, Norwich, Oneida, and Oswego.

At Port Jervis, N. Y., with the Port Jervis and Monticello Railroad for Monticello, N. Y. Also with stage for Milford, Pa., and all points in the lower Delaware Valley.

At Hawley, Pa. (*via* Honesdale Branch from Lackawaxen), with the Pennsylvania Coal Company's Gravity Railroad for Scranton, Pa., Pittston, Pa., Wilkesbarre, Pa., and all points in Pennsylvania Coal Regions.

At Honesdale, Pa. (*via* Honesdale Branch from Lackawaxen), with Delaware and Hudson Canal Company's Gravity Road for Carbondale, Pa., Scranton, Pa., and all points in Pennsylvania Coal Regions.

At Binghamton, N. Y., with the Albany and Susquehanna Railroad for Cooperstown, Sharon Springs, Albany, Troy, Saratoga, Boston, and principal New England cities; Syracuse and Binghamtom Railroad for Syracuse and Oswego, and for Utica and Richfield Springs *via* Utica, Chenango, and Susquehanna Valley Railroad from Chenango Forks; Southern Central Railroad for Auburn; Delaware, Lackawanna, and Western Railroad for Scranton.

At Owego, N. Y., with Cayuga Division, Delaware, Lackawanna, and Western Railroad for Ithaca and Cayuga Lake.

At Elmira, N. Y., with Northern Central Railroad for Watkins Glen, Penn Yann, and Canandaigua, Williamsport, Harrisburg, Philadelphia, Baltimore, and Washington; Lehigh Valley Railroad for Wilkesbarre, Mauch Chunk, Easton, and Philadelphia; Utica, Ithaca, and Elmira Railroad for Ithaca and Syracuse; Tioga and State Line Railroad for Tioga and Blossburg, Pa., and points in the semi-bituminous coal field of Pennsylvania.

At Corning, N. Y., with Corning, Cowanesque, and Antrim Railroad for Tioga, Wellsboro', and Antrim, Pa., and points in semi-bituminous coal fields; Syracuse, Geneva, and Corning Railroad for Dundee and Geneva, N. Y.

At Bath, N. Y. (*via* Rochester Division from Corning), with Bath and Hammondsport Railroad, for Hammondsport and Penn Yann, *via* Keuka Lake steamers from Hammondsport.

At Gainesville, N. Y. (*via* Buffalo Division from Hornellsville), with Silver Lake Railway for Perry on Silver Lake.

## ERIE RAILWAY ROUTE.

At Wellsville, N. Y., and Cuba, N. Y., with the Bradford, Eldred, and Cuba Narrow Gauge Railroad for Bolivar, Smethport, and all points in the Alleghany oil field, Eldred, Pa., and *via* the Bradford, Bordell, and Kinzua Narrow Gauge from Eldred for Kane, Pa.

At Cuba, N. Y., with Richburg Branch of Bradford, Eldred, and Cuba Railroad for Richburg, and with Tonawanda Valley Railroad for Java, Arcade and Attica, N. Y.

At Olean, N. Y., with Buffalo, New York and Philadelphia Railway for Buffalo, N. Y., Emporium, Ridgway, Lockhaven, Williamsport, Sunbury, Hamburg and Philadelphia, Pa., Baltimore and Washington, and points in Northern Oil Fields.

At Salamanca, N. Y., with Rochester and Pittsburgh Railroad for LeRoy, Warsaw, and Rochester, and the New York, Pennsylvania, and Ohio Railroad for Jamestown, Chautauqua Lake, and points in the middle and lower Oil Regions.

### THROUGH CONNECTIONS.

At Buffalo, with the Grand Trunk and Great Western Railways of Canada, and the Lake Shore and Michigan Southern R. R., making close connection with the entire system of railroads traversing the great West, and running direct to Cleveland, Cincinnati, Detroit, Chicago, St. Louis, and all points in the West, Northwest, South, and Southwest. Connection is also made with the steamers which, traversing the chain of immense lakes on our northern frontier, call at every port from Buffalo to Duluth, at the head of Lake Superior.

At Salamanca with the New York, Pennsylvania, and Ohio Railroad for Cleveland, Cincinnati, Chicago, St. Louis, and all points West. This is the route of the famous "Erie and Chicago line," which runs Pullman Palace, Hotel, Sleeping, and Drawing-room cars without change between New York and Chicago, and of the St. Louis "Limited" Express, running Pullman Sleeping Coaches through to Cincinnati and St. Louis.

At Dunkirk, with the Lake Shore and Michigan Southern R. R.

It will be seen that the traveler, either for business or pleasure, has almost unlimited facilities for reaching every part of the country *via* the Erie Railway, and a choice of routes in so doing.

The points along the main line, from which the various branches and divisions diverge, together with the stations upon each, will be noted in their proper places in the succeeding pages of this Guide

## ERIE RAILWAY ROUTE.

and they are brought together here in order that the traveler may see, at a glance, the constant and ever-active enterprise of the Erie Railway Company in extending facilities for traffic and travel into the country adjacent to their main line.

The equipment necessary to provide facilities for the constantly increasing travel and freight business of this road is something enormous. At the present time there are owned and in use five hundred and thirty-nine locomotives, four hundred regular passenger, mail, express, and baggage cars, and twenty-three thousand freight, coal, stock, and oil-cars. In addition to all these there are the Pullman Palace, Drawing-room, Dining, and Sleeping Coaches, elegantly furnished, in which traveling changes from a fatigue into a positive delight.

### SCENERY, ETC.

The scenery along the route is eminently grand and imposing. After passing through the picturesque valley of the Passaic, in Northern New Jersey, and the rolling and verdure-clad pastures of Rockland and Orange Counties, where some of the finest dairies in the world are found, the bold and rugged scenery of the Delaware valley engages the attention of the traveler for the next 100 miles, to Deposit Station. From here we cross the country, surmounting a summit, to the Susquehanna valley. The valley of this beautiful river and its tributaries is then followed to Hornellsville, affording interesting and picturesque views of scenery, more particularly mentioned in the descriptions of the different stations. From Hornellsville, on the main route, we again strike across the country, surmounting another summit, to the Alleghany River, at Olean, and follow its valley to Salamanca, from thence up the wild and rugged one of a tributary stream, and over another summit, to the basin of Lake Erie, in descending the slope of which we catch occasional glimpses of that remarkable inland sea.

The Erie Railway in the course of its route brings the traveler within easy distance of each one of that singular tier of lakes which lie across the central portion of Western New York. These bodies of water, varying in extent, but all of considerable size, are a marked feature in the topography of the State. They all have a general direction north and south, and, navigable for steamboats, are surrounded by

## ERIE RAILWAY ROUTE.

lands of great fertility, abound in fish, and on several of them the scenery is remarkably beautiful. Beginning with the most easterly, we have Skaneateles Lake, Owasco Lake, Cayuga Lake, Seneca Lake, Crooked Lake, Canandaigua Lake, Honeoye Lake, Canadice Lake, Hemlock Lake, and Conesus Lake. The six first-named drain their waters by the Oswego River, and the remainder by the Genesee River into Lake Ontario. In several of these lakes the water is of great depth and wonderful purity. In Seneca Lake the bottom can be distinctly seen at a depth of thirty feet; and soundings have been made which show in some places a depth of 500 feet. The larger of these lakes rarely freeze over their entire surfaces; more or less clear water being visible except in the most extraordinarily severe winters. Being easily reached from various points on the Erie or its branches, and the larger ones having facilities for navigation, they are yearly visited by an increasing number of tourists. The points on the Erie Railway from which these lakes can be most conveniently reached are as follows: For Skaneateles Lake, Binghamton; for Cayuga Lake, Owego; for Seneca Lake, Elmira; for Crooked Lake, Bath; for Canandaigua Lake, Blood's Station; for Conesus, Hemlock, Canadice, and Honeoye Lakes, Livonia. At each of these points the tourist will find either rail or stage communications. Beyond the Genesee we have Silver Lake, in Wyoming County, and at last the beautiful Chautauqua, "the gem of New York lakes," whose waters turn southward through the Alleghany River, the Ohio, and the Mississippi.

### TRAFFIC ON THE ERIE RAILWAY.

The extraordinary multiplication of connecting routes has had its legitimate result in developing the business of the Erie Railway. The iron, coal, lumber, and oil of Northern Pennsylvania, the grain and live stock of the vast western prairies, the dairy products of New York and Ohio, the returning freights of merchandise from the great metropolis, furnish a traffic sufficient to make the revenues of a kingdom ; while the vast increase in the passenger business, as compared with other trunk lines, furnishes unerring testimony that the superior comforts and attractions of this route are being more and more understood and appreciated by the traveling public. The annual report of the New York State Engineer for 1881 makes public the important official fact that the Erie Railway carried 5,491,441 passengers during that year, and that out of that number only two were killed, both of them through their own carelessness. Volumes could not demonstrate more completely the attractions and conveniences of a road that induce such an enormous army of tourists to select it, nor the constant care of a management which renders the transportation of them so secure.

Passengers intending to travel by the Erie from New York have only to leave their orders at the offices of the Company, when an agent will call for their baggage and check it direct from hotel or residence to destination. An agent passes through the cars and takes up checks for baggage from the incoming passengers, delivering it to whatever part of New York or Brooklyn it may be ordered sent.

Broadway, New York,
LOOKING SOUTH FROM BARCLAY STREET AND THE NEW POST OFFICE.

THE BROOKLYN BRIDGE.

ERIE RAILWAY ROUTE.

**JERSEY CITY, Hudson Co., N. J.,**

*1 mile from New York. From Dunkirk, 459.*

The second largest city in the State of New Jersey, having a population of about 120,000, and the seat of a large manufacturing interest. It contains many churches, seminaries, and public schools of unusual excellence; banks, savings institutions, etc , etc., and many elegant private residences. The position of the city is one of extraordinary advantage, being the initial point of several important lines of railway to the West and South. The Pennsylvania Central, the New Jersey Central, the New Jersey Midland, and the Delaware, Lackawanna, and Western R.R., all have their main depots here. The city has a large frontage on two very deep rivers—the Hudson and the Hackensack—and a large and growing shipping interest. Two lines of ocean steamers have their docks here: the Monarch, to Liverpool, and the New York and Cardiff line to Wales.

Leaving Jersey City, the Bergen Tunnel is soon reached. This tunnel is cut through Bergen Heights, the southern end of a remarkable ridge of land lying parallel to the Hudson River, and between it and the great salt marsh through which the Hackensack River flows into Newark Bay. The eastern side of this ridge is a line of precipitous cliffs called the Palisades, which, extending through Jersey City, strike the Hudson River at Weehawken, and form its west bank for more than twenty miles, nearly to Piermont. The tunnel is about seven-eighths of a mile in length, and was completed in 1861. On the height of land a few rods north of the tunnel is the reservoir from which Jersey City is supplied with water, which is brought in pipes from the Passaic River. Just after emerging from the tunnel, the Nyack branch, or Northern R.R. of New Jersey, diverges to the right (see p. 73), and the Newark branch (see p. 72) to the left. The main line crosses the salt marsh and the Hackensack River, and the first station is

**RUTHERFORD PARK, Bergen Co., N. J.,**

*9½ miles from New York. From Dunkirk, 450½.*

Here is a thriving suburban village of about 600 inhabitants, situated within the limits of Union Township. The residents chiefly carry on business in New York city. The village contains several churches, a good school, several summer boarding-houses, and a large hotel. Fine fishing, boating, and hunting are among the attractions of this place. The drives are delightful. Two miles west of Rutherford Park the railroad crosses Passaic River, a beautiful stream, flowing south through the city of Newark into Newark Bay, affording an outlet for navigation from Newark to New York.

### PASSAIC, Passaic Co., N. J.,
$12\frac{1}{2}$ *miles from New York. From Dunkirk,* $447\frac{1}{2}$.

This is a large and handsome place, having a population of about 5,000. The village is beautifully laid out, and is rendered attractive by an abundance of shade trees. There are a number of churches, two good hotels, many private houses which entertain summer visitors, and several large manufactories located in the village and its suburbs. Dundee Lake, 3 miles distant, is reached by a charming drive.

### CLIFTON, Passaic Co., N. J.,
$13\frac{1}{4}$ *miles from New York. From Dunkirk,* $446\frac{1}{4}$.

This is a small but attractive place, near the shores of Dundee Lake, a noted resort for lovers of fishing and aquatic sports. Many prominent New York business men have their residences here. Drives to Paterson, Passaic, Rutherford, Hackensack, and Belleville are very charming.

### LAKE VIEW, Passaic Co., N. J.,
15 *miles from New York. From Dunkirk,* 445. *Hotel Lake View.*

Pleasantly situated on a slope of ground rising eastward from the railway track to a considerable eminence, whence it overlooks the Passaic River and Dundee Lake, and a charming variety of landscape.

### PATERSON, Passaic Co., N. J.,
17 *miles from New York. From Dunkirk,* 443.

This city, one of the largest in the State, contains about 50,000 inhabitants. It was founded in 1791, under the auspices of Alexander Hamilton, for the purpose of carrying on the cotton manufacture. The place has become an important manufacturing city, having an immense water-power, and good facilities for communication with the great markets. Besides the Erie Railway, the Del., Lack., and Western R.R., the New Jersey Midland R.R., and the

ERIE RAILWAY ROUTE.

Morris Canal pass through the city. It is also connected with Newark by a branch of the Erie. The Grant and Rogers Locomotive Works, silk mills, and numerous factories have made the place famous the world over. The celebrated Passaic Falls are within the limits of the city, and the scenery in the neighborhood is bold and romantic. There are several places for the accommodation of the traveler.

**HAWTHORNE, Passaic Co., N. J.,**
*19 miles from New York. From Dunkirk, 441.*
A thickly settled suburb of Paterson. Close at hand are the Preakness Hills, the "Goffle," and the historic Waugarau Valley, where the Indians came to meet the old Dutch settlers and enjoy the first "waugan raucht," or wagon ride. This locality abounds in traditions of interest to the antiquarian.

**RIDGEWOOD, Bergen Co., N. J.,**
*22 miles from New York. From Dunkirk, 438.*
The village, formerly called Godwinville Station, is situated on the eastern slope of a wooded ridge, and spreads over the fairest part of the Paramus Valley. Several celebrated men reside here. There are some points of historical interest near here. The location is free from all malaria, and healthful.

**HOHOKUS, Bergen Co., N. J.,**
*23¼ miles from New York. From Dunkirk, 436¼.*
The location is romantic and picturesque. On the one side is a wild gorge through which a torrent rapidly rushes; on the other stretches the fairest portion of the Paramus Valley. Directly below the station is the old stone mansion in which Aaron Burr wooed and won Miss Provost. Farther away is the Dutch Church, turned by the British into a prison-house for soldiers of the Revolutionary army. Hohokus is the residence of Joe Jefferson, the famous Rip Van Winkle.

**ALLENDALE, Bergen Co., N. J.,**
*25¾ miles from New York. From Dunkirk, 434¼.*
Noted for the extent of its fruit and berry culture; within a short distance are several churches of various denominations.

VIEW ON THE ERIE RAILWAY AT HOHOKUS.

ERIE RAILWAY ROUTE.

**RAMSEY'S, Bergen Co., N. J.,**
28 *miles from New York.   From Dunkirk,* 432.

This village has long been famed for the quantity of strawberries it sends to the New York market. There are two hotels, and a number of summer boarding-houses. Within a short distance are eight churches. Darlington, the celebrated stock farm of the proprietor of the Fifth Avenue Hotel, is near Ramsey's.

**MAHWAH, Bergen Co., N. J.,**
30 *miles from New York.   From Dunkirk,* 430.

The enchanting scenery of this neighborhood offers great attractions to the summer visitor.

**SUFFERN, Rockland Co., N. Y.,**
32 *miles from New York.   From Dunkirk,* 428.

At this point the traveler finds himself at the base of a range of mountains named the Ramapo or Blue Mountains. They are properly the southern extremity of the Highlands of the Hudson. Suffern is the beginning of the beautiful scenery of the Ramapo Valley. In the immediate neighborhood are lakes abounding in bass and pickerel. There are good hotels and private boarding-houses, and churches of various denominations.

From Suffern the old line of the Erie diverges through Tallman's, Monsey, Spring Valley, Nanuet, and Blauveltsville, all of which, except Spring Valley, are small and unimportant stations, to

**PIERMONT, Rockland Co., N. Y.,**
24 *miles from New York.   From Dunkirk,* 446.

This place is beautifully situated on the west bank of the Hudson, a little above the upper end of the Palisades, and on the lower end of the widening in the river known as Tappan Bay. The views in all directions—up, down, and across the river, and towards the Highlands in the rear—are very attractive, and Piermont has become a popular place of summer residence for many of the citizens of New York. Near Tarrytown, on the opposite side of the river, is the place where André was captured, and the place of his execution was at Tappan, the village shown on the map a little southwest of

FALLS OF THE RAMAPO RIVER.

## ERIE RAILWAY ROUTE.

Piermont. An immense pier, one mile in length, extends out into the river at the terminus of the railway, and with the mountain in the rear of the village gives the name of Piermont to the town.

---

The railway now passes through a deep valley, or gap, in the range of hills which cross this country in a south-westerly direction, extending from the Highlands of the Hudson across into New Jersey, where they form the Orange Mountain. A short distance beyond Suffern are the remains of a fortification thrown up in the Revolutionary war to defend the pass from an anticipated advance of the British towards New York. This whole region is peculiarly rich in revolutionary relics and lore.

### RAMAPO, Rockland Co., N. Y.,
*34 miles from New York. From Dunkirk, 426.*

An extensive car-building and car-wheel manufacturing interest is located at this point. The Ramapo Manufacturing Co., and the Ramapo Wheel and Foundry Co., are among the largest car and carwheel factories in the country. A prominent feature of the landscape here is Torne Mountain, from the summit of which General Washington watched the movements of the British troops in New York harbor, while he was quartered in the Ramapo Valley.

### SLOATSBURG, Rockland Co., N. Y.,
*36 miles from New York. From Dunkirk, 424.*

An attractive village, with beautiful scenery all around it. Many lakes in the neighborhood afford sport for the angler.

### LORILLARD'S, Rockland Co., N. Y.,
*38¼ miles from New York. From Dunkirk, 421½.*

This is a station for the accommodation of visitors to Lorillard Lake, one of a dozen or more mountain lakes in this region. It is the property of the Lorillards in New York, and a great resort for black bass fishermen.

### SOUTHFIELDS, Orange Co., N. Y.,
*42 miles from New York. From Dunkirk, 418.*

A station surrounded by mountain scenery.

ERIE RAILWAY ROUTE.

### GREENWOOD, Orange Co., N. Y.,
*44 miles from New York.   From Dunkirk,* 416.

Here are located the extensive furnaces in which are manufactured the materials for the famous Parrott guns.

### TURNER'S, Orange Co., N. Y.,
*48 miles from New York.   From Dunkirk,* 412.

Change cars for Central Valley, Highland Mills, Woodbury, Mountainville, Cornwall, and Newburg.

Here is the beginning of the famous Orange county dairy region. There is a very well kept eating-house at this station, at which all trains stop for refreshments. The village is a mere hamlet. It is one of the most popular refreshment stations on the route. Slaughter, Rumsey, Little Long, Mambasha, and Round lakes are within three or four miles of this place. From Turner's diverges the short cut to Newburg (see p. 75).

### MONROE, Orange Co., N. Y.,
*50 miles from New York.   From Dunkirk,* 410.

HOTELS: SEVEN SPRINGS MOUNTAIN HOUSE, AND MONROE HOUSE.

This village has the greatest altitude above tide-water between Jersey City and the Shawangunk Mountains. The adjacent country is a famous dairy section, and immense quantities of milk are sent from this station to New York. Several handsome lakes are in the vicinity. Greenwood Lake is nine miles distant, and Monroe, Mambasha, Walton, and Long ponds, abounding in fish, are near.

### OXFORD, Orange Co., N. Y.,
*52 miles from New York.   From Dunkirk,* 408.

A small hamlet, near which an iron mine is worked, the ore being sent to the works at Greenwood. There are eight churches within three miles.

### GREYCOURT, Orange Co., N. Y.,
*54 miles from New York.   From Dunkirk,* 406.

This is quite a railroad centre; for from this point diverge two branch roads, one to Warwick (see p. 76), ten miles south, the other to Newburgh. Prior to the completion of the "Short Cut," the latter was the regularly traveled Erie route to that city. It is eighteen miles in length, and follows the valley of Moodna (Murderer's) Creek, passing Craigville, Washington, Salisbury, and Vail's Gate stations, through a hilly country, though the hills are generally arable to their summits. Three-fourths of a mile beyond Vail's Gate, a junction is made with the "Short Cut Line," to Newburgh.

Passing Greycourt, we soon cross the Greycourt Meadows, a curious peat-bog nearly a hundred feet in depth in some parts, so soft and yielding that it was found necessary to make a foundation for the railway by driving piles to prevent the earth embankment from being swallowed up as fast as deposited. The bones of a large mastodon were found in this bog some years ago. The soil is very fertile, having been reclaimed by draining, etc., and immense crops of onions are raised here.

### CHESTER, Orange Co., N. Y.,
*55 miles from New York. From Dunkirk, 405.*

This is the name of the township and of its central village. The railway runs through East Chester, and there is another village called West Chester; the three villages being arranged in a triangle about a mile apart.

### GOSHEN, Orange Co., N. Y.,
*61 miles from New York. From Dunkirk, 399.*

A beautiful village of about 2,500 inhabitants, and lies in the heart of Orange County. The dairies in this region are celebrated. Until the farmers adopted the plan of selling the milk in the New York market instead of making it into butter, "Goshen butter" was famous the country over. The Minisink monument, in the public square, commemorates the gallant men who fell fighting the noted Indian leader Brandt ("Thay-an-den-egea, the Scourge"), in 1779. The traveler will find churches, banks, newspapers, and all the modern improvements in this pleasant town. At and near Goshen are some of the largest horse-breeding establishments in the world; near by are also the stock farms of Robert Bonner, Goldsmith, and others. Goshen is well situated for a place of summer resort, as famous fishing and hunting grounds are within easy reach. The hotels and boarding-houses are numerous and well appointed. From Goshen two branches of the Erie diverge, the Montgomery branch (see p. 78), and the Pine Island branch (see p. 77).

Change cars for Montgomery, Lake Mohonk, Lake Minnewaska (New Paltz), and resorts in the Catskill Mountains.

ERIE RAILWAY ROUTE.

## HAMPTON, Orange Co., N. Y.,
*64 miles from New York. From Dunkirk, 396.*

Prior to the diversion of the water-power of the Wallkill River, this was a maufacturing town, but is now a quiet village. The valley of the Wallkill is chiefly made up of peat-bogs, large portions of which have been drained and proved to be remarkably fertile. Bones of the mastodon have been found in these bogs.

## MIDDLETOWN, Orange Co., N. Y.,
*67 miles from New York. From Dunkirk, 393.*

Situated between and upon a number of sloping hills facing each other, like the seats in an amphitheatre, is an important and growing place. The scenery on every side is enchanting, and presents many attractions to the tourist. The city has a number of churches, some of which are noble structures, and many elegant private dwellings. The State Homœopathic Asylum for the insane is located here. There are a number of good hotels. The manufacturing interests are large, and embrace a considerable variety of products, among which are, steel, saws, files, horse-shoe nails, hats, blankets, leather, agricultural implements, etc. Over a thousand hands are employed in these industries. There are excellent schools, several banks and newspapers, waterworks, and a good Fire Department. Population about 9,000. The Crawford branch of the Erie extends from Middletown through a rich dairy region to Pine Bush, near the Ulster County line. The New York, Ontario, and Western R.R. diverges from Middletown, running a northerly course to Oswego on Lake Ontario, and the New Jersey Midland southerly through New Jersey to New York city.

## HOWELL'S, Orange Co., N. Y.,
*71 miles from New York. From Dunkirk, 389.*

A small village. Beyond Howell's some of the finest scenery on the route begins. The railway leaves the fertile meadows of Orange Co., and begins the ascent of the Shawangunk range, the cultivated lands disappear, and Nature in wild beauty resumes her empire.

ON THE UPPER DELAWARE RIVER.

ERIE RAILWAY ROUTE.

### OTISVILLE, Orange Co., N. Y.,
*76 miles from New York. From Dunkirk, 384.*

Otisville is nearly on the summit of the mountain. Passing through a long and heavy rock cut, the summit is passed, and the valley below is reached by gradually descending the steep and rugged slope of the Shawangunk mountain, in a southerly direction, on a grade of about forty-five feet to a mile. The character of the scenery changes wonderfully after leaving Otisville. We pass alternately through gloomy cuts and over side-hill embankments, commanding magnificent views of the romantic valley of the Neversink, traversed by the Delaware and Hudson Canal, and dotted with farm-houses and villages.

### GUYMARD, Orange Co., N. Y.,
*80 miles from New York. From Dunkirk, 380.*

There is a fine hotel, a chalybeate spring, and a clear mountain lake well supplied with fish, affording, in connection with a healthful atmosphere and mountain scenery, a popular summer retreat near the metropolis. Near the base of the mountain the railroad passes through the "Black Rock Cut," then describes a long curve commanding a beautiful view of the Delaware and Neversink Valleys.

### PORT JERVIS, Orange Co., N. Y.,
*88 miles from New York. From Dunkirk, 372.*

Stands upon the eastern bank of the Delaware, overshadowed by the twin mountains Point Peter and Mount William. Port Jervis is one of the most flourishing towns on the line of the Erie Railway. At a point just south of the town, near the junction of the Neversink with the Delaware, is the corner boundary between New York, Pennsylvania, and New Jersey. Port Jervis was so named in honor of John B. Jervis, the engineer of the Delaware and Hudson Canal. There are three good hotels, churches of various denominations, and a population of about ten thousand. Port Jervis is the station from which the picturesque summer resorts, Milford and Dingman's, in Pike County, Pa., are reached by stage and carriage over one of the finest drives in the county. The scenery about these places is unrivaled. Numerous lakes and waterfalls are to be found in the immediate vicinity; deer and other wild game

## ERIE RAILWAY ROUTE.

afford sport to the hunter, while the streams are stocked with black and striped bass, trout, etc. De Witt Clinton, whose name is inseparably linked with the great system of internal improvements in the State of New York, was born near Port Jervis.

VIEW ON THE ERIE RAILWAY, DELAWARE RIVER.

Stages run daily to Milford, Dingman's Ferry, and Stroudsburg, Pa., and to Branchville, N. J., connecting there with the Sussex R.R. for Newton, etc. From Port Jervis the Port Jervis and Monticello Railway extends into the famous Sullivan County summer resort region, the terminus being Monticello, 24 miles (see p. 78). This is the route from New York to White Lake.

**POND EDDY, Pike Co., Pa.,**
*100 miles from New York. From Dunkirk, 360.*
The name of a point in the river where a sudden bend forms a wide

AQUADUCT
OF THE
DELAWARE AND HUDSON CANAL,
ACROSS THE DELAWARE RIVER, AT
LACKAWAXEN, PA.

ERIE RAILWAY ROUTE.

and deep basin. The road runs for a long distance along the steep and rugged bank of the Delaware, high up the side of the precipice. The view, though perhaps trying to the nerves of a timorous man, especially when flying along on the lightning express train, is grand and imposing. This portion of the road was extremely difficult and expensive to build, being cut in the solid rock. It was frequently necessary, in making the surveys, to lower the engineers and their assistants from above with ropes to prevent them from falling.

### SHOHOLA, Pike Co., Pa.,
*107 miles from New York. From Dunkirk, 353.*

Opposite to this station is the village of Barryville, in Sullivan County, N. Y., supported principally by the coal and lumber trade On the Shohola Creek, a mile from the station, is a wonderful glen, abounding in waterfalls and weird nooks. Shohola is the station for a celebrated game and fishing region in Sullivan and Pike counties. Six miles from Shohola, in Sullivan County, are the Highland Lakes, a favorite summer resort.

### LACKAWAXEN, Pike Co., Pa.,
*111 miles from New York. From Dunkirk, 349.*

At the junction of Lackawaxen and Delaware rivers. The Delaware and Hudson Canal comes down the valley of the Lackawaxen River, and crosses the Delaware River in an aqueduct supported by a wire suspension bridge. The Honesdale branch (see page 79) here unites with the Erie Railway, bringing in the immense quantities of anthracite coal which are mined and forwarded by the Pennsylvania Coal Co. and Delaware and Hudson Canal Co. Lackawaxen is a favorite summer resort for city people. There are the best of trout, bass and pickerel fishing here, and deer and partridge hunting. Near by, on the hill overlooking the Delaware, was fought, in 1779, the bloody battle of Minisink, between the Indians, under Brandt, and the American militia, under Colonel Tusten, in which the militia suffered severely, about one-half of them being killed. Until very lately it was possible to find, imbedded in the forest trees that were standing at the time of the conflict, bullets that had been fired by the participants in the battle. The whole region was a favorite hunting-ground of the Indians, and many relics, such as arrowheads and tomahawks,

ERIE RAILWAY ROUTE.

have been found. Five miles from Lackawaxen, in the primeval woods, are the ruins of the buildings of Horace Greeley's unsuccessful Fourierite Community.

### PINE GROVE, Pike Co., Pa.,

116 *miles from New York. From Dunkirk*, 344.

A small, unimportant station, two miles beyond which the railway recrosses the Delaware over a wooden bridge about 600 feet long.

### NARROWSBURG, Sullivan Co., N. Y.,

122 *miles from New York. From Dunkirk*, 338.

So called from the narrow gorge through which the river passes at this place. A wooden bridge connects the two banks by a single span of 184 feet. A pretty village, and quite popular as a summer residence. Narrowsburg is a leading dining station on the Erie, express trains stopping twenty minutes here for meals.

### COCHECTON, Sullivan Co., N. Y.,

131 *miles from New York. From Dunkirk*, 329.

A rich valley, about two miles long and one mile wide, here stretches along the river, abounding in orchards, grain fields, and meadows. On the other side of the river, in Pennsylvania, is the village of Damascus. In this locality is laid the scene of Cooper's novel, "The Last of the Mohicans."

### CALLICOON, Sullivan Co., N. Y.,

136 *miles from New York. From Dunkirk*, 324.

On Callicoon Creek, the region is wild and thinly settled. The inhabitants are engaged in lumbering, farming and tanning.

### HANKINS, Sullivan Co., N. Y.,

143 *miles from New York. From Dunkirk*, 317.

A small, unimportant station near the line of Sullivan County.

### BASKET STATION, Sullivan Co., N. Y.,

143 *miles from New York. From Dunkirk*, 317.

At the mouth of Basket Creek. The post-office is Long Eddy.

OLD BRIDGE OVER THE DELAWARE AT NARROWSBURG, N. Y.

ERIE RAILWAY ROUTE.

### LORDVILLE, Delaware Co., N. Y.,

154 *miles from New York.*   *From Dunkirk*, 306.

Formerly called Equinunk Station, from the pretty village of that name on the opposite side of the river in Pennsylvania.

### STOCKPORT, Delaware Co., N. Y.,

159 *miles from New York.*   *From Dunkirk*, 301.

The village of Stockport is across the river in Pennsylvania. Four miles north of here the railroad crosses the east branch of the Delaware, which unites with the main branch a little below.

### HANCOCK, Delaware Co., N. Y.,

164 *miles from New York.*   *From Dunkirk*, 296.

This pretty, romantic village, shut in between the mountains, is at the junction of the two branches of the Delaware; it is an important railroad and trading station. A suspension bridge spans the Delaware at this place.

### HALE'S EDDY, Delaware Co., N. Y.,

172 *miles from New York.*   *From Dunkirk*, 288.

So named from Oliver Hale, the first settler.

### DEPOSIT, Delaware Co., N. Y.,

177 *miles from New York.*   *From Dunkirk*, 283.

Formerly the center of a large lumber business; is an important station. Extensive cattle-yards were erected here in 1870. One mile west of this point we cross the Oquago Creek, and leaving the basin of the Delaware, commence on a heavy ascending grade to surmount the dividing ridge between this basin and that of the Susquehanna. For eight miles the road passes through wild and rugged scenery, with occasional magnificent views.

### SUMMIT, Broome Co., N, Y.,

185 *miles from New York.*   *From Dunkirk*, 275.

This station is 1,366 feet above the level of the sea. Deposit being 997 feet above, a difference of 369 feet in eight miles. From this

SCENE ON THE UPPER DELAWARE.

point the road descends on a grade of sixty feet per mile for about eight miles. About four miles from the summit we come to the Cascade Bridge, a beautiful and wonderful structure, spanning a ravine 250 feet wide and 184 feet deep. A very inadequate idea of its magnitude can be formed while passing over it in the cars; but from the valley below, the view is truly magnificent. The bridge is constructed of wood and iron, and though very strong and solid, arches between the natural abutments of solid rock in a light and graceful manner. It was constructed under the direction of John Fowler.

STARUCCA VIADUCT—ERIE RAILWAY.

Shortly after leaving this bridge we arrive at the Starucca Viaduct. This is a little beyond the State line in Pennsylvania. It is a magnificent and costly structure, 1,200 feet in length and 110 feet in height. There are eighteen arches. Like the Cascade Bridge, it should be viewed from below to obtain a full idea of its grandeur and extent. By stopping over one train at the next station, Susquehanna, this may easily be accomplished. The village of Lanesborough is passed, a little beyond the viaduct, on a trestle bridge, some seventy feet above the Caneawacta Creek.

### SUSQUEHANNA, Susquehanna Co., Pa.,

*193 miles from New York. From Dunkirk, 267.*

At this place the Railway Company have established very extensive repair-shops and engine-houses, giving employment to a large number of men. Meals are supplied to travelers at the spacious dining-saloon at the station.

The road now follows the valley of the Susquehanna, crossing it on a wooden bridge, 800 feet long, half a mile beyond the station. The grades are now very light, not exceeding five feet per mile on the entire Susquehanna section, extending to Hornellsville.

From Susquehanna a branch road passes through Susquehanna Co., Pa., to the heart of the great anthracite region in Luzerne Co. The distance from Susquehanna to Carbondale, its terminus, is 38 miles. This road is one of the great feeders of the Erie, pouring a constant and enormous coal tonnage, *via* the main line, to tide water at Jersey City, and westward to Binghamton and points north.

### GREAT BEND, Susquehanna Co., Pa.,

*201 miles from New York. From Dunkirk, 259.*

The village of Great Bend, on the opposite side of the river from the station, is connected with a bridge for ordinary travel. Running four miles northwesterly from Great Bend, the railway crosses into New York State once more and does not again leave it.

### KIRKWOOD, Broome Co., N. Y.,

*206 miles from New York. From Dunkirk, 254.*

Named after the former able Superintendent of the road. Near this place is the birthplace of the celebrated Joe Smith, the great original prophet of the Mormon religion.

ERIE RAILWAY ROUTE.

**BINGHAMTON, Broome Co., N. Y.**
216 *miles from New York.  From Dunkirk,* 244.
HOTEL : HOTEL BENNETT.

This beautiful city, incorporated in 1867, is delightfully situated at the junction of the Chenango and Susquehanna rivers, and is one of the finest inland cities in the State. Its broad and well-paved streets, handsome church edifices and business structures, bear evidence of prosperity and wealth. Besides the Erie, five other railroads centre here. The Albany and Susquehanna, giving direct communication with Albany, Saratoga Springs, Boston, and the principal New England cities, and also with Carbondale and Scranton, and points in the anthracite coal fields ; the Delaware, Lackawanna, and Western for Scranton, the Pennsylvania coal regions, Delaware Water Gap, and Philadelphia ; the Syracuse and Binghamton R.R. for Syracuse and Oswego ; the Utica and Chenango Valley R.R. for Norwich, Richfield Springs, Utica, etc.

The State Insane Asylum is located here, two and a half miles east of the city, north of the railway, on the crest of a hill commanding a magnificent view of the Susquehanna Valley, the city, and the surrounding country. It is 365 feet long and 82 feet wide, and is built of stone and brick, in the castellated Gothic style of architecture. Its grounds occupy about 400 acres. The Susquehanna Valley Home and Industrial School for indigent children opened Sept. 7, 1870. It is on the south side of the Susquehanna river on a tract of 45 acres, and has received State aid towards its support. There are several academies, a High School for both sexes, a commercial college, several hotels, and newspapers, numerous fine and costly churches, extensive manufacturing interests and a large and growing local trade. On account of the extraordinary facilities for bringing together here the iron and coal products of the whole country, its available water-power, good climate, and attractive natural surroundings, Binghamton offers great inducements as a location for manufacturing interests. The city has a population of 21,000. In 1870 it had less than 13,000 ; this growth is the result of the development of business enterprises.

**HOOPER, Broome Co., N. Y.**
221 *miles from New York.  From Dunkirk,* 239.

A small village at the mouth of Patterson Creek. The Methodist Episcopal Church has here two groves for camp-meetings.

HEAD WATERS CAYUGA LAKE, N.Y.

ERIE RAILWAY ROUTE.

### UNION, Broome Co., N. Y.
*223 miles from New York. From Dunkirk, 237*

A flourishing village in the township of the same name, about half a mile from the Susquehanna River, surrounded by fine farming lands. There are three hotels, a large tannery, and several lumber establishments and rake factories. Stage connections are made to Maine, Broome Co., to Whitney's Point, Union Center, Glen Aubrey, and Lamb's Corners daily. Crossing Nanticoke Creek, the road turns to the north and passes the manufacturing village of Apalachin.

### CAMPVILLE, Tioga Co., N. Y.
*230 miles from New York. From Dunkirk, 230.*

A small village just half-way between New York and Dunkirk.

### OWEGO, Tioga Co., N. Y.
*237 miles from New York. From Dunkirk, 223.*

HOTEL: AHWAGA. This is the county seat of Tioga County. It is situated at the junction of Owego Creek and the Susquehanna River. The village is rapidly increasing in importance, and now has about 6,000 population, and is the center of a large agricultural district. The county buildings are among the finest in the State. Among the prominent business enterprises are the "Champion" Grain Drill Co., the Owego Cruciform Burial Casket Co., and Ely's Cream Balm for cartarrhal troubles, which ranks high as a curative, and is for sale by druggists throughout the United States.

Beautiful drives are numerous about Owego. A bridge connects the two banks of the Susquehanna. On the Owego Creek, in the west part of the village, is "Glen Mary," the former residence of N. P. Willis. Here he wrote his charming "Letters from under a Bridge."

Connection is made at Owego with the Southern Central Railroad for Auburn. The Cayuga Division of the Delaware, Lackawanna, and Western Railroad extends from Owego to Ithaca on Cayuga Lake, affording a direct and easy route from New York, *via* the Erie, to one of the most picturesque regions in the State.

Stages run daily to Flemingville, Weltonville, West Newark, Jenksville, and Speedville, and tri-weekly to Apalachin, Little Meadows, Friendsville, West Warren, and Le Raysville.

A steamboat runs on the Susquehanna River to Hiawatha Grove, a **noted picnic ground four miles east of Owego.**

ERIE RAILWAY ROUTE.

**ITHACA,** Tompkins Co., **N. Y.,**
269 *miles from New York.*
HOTEL: ITHACA HOUSE.

This place is not directly on the line of the Erie Railway, yet its importance and attractiveness to the tourist require for it a place in this work, especially as the Erie is the chief means of approach from New York and the east and west to this delightful resort of the lover

ENFIELD FALLS, NEAR ITHACA, N. Y.

of nature. Owing to the peculiar formation of the rock strata in this region the streams have worn deep channels, and waterfalls which were once at the face of the bluffs have receded from one to two miles, forming deep rocky chasms, bordered by perpendicular walls. As the rocks are composed of strata differing in hardness, the water has worn them irregularly.

## ERIE RAILWAY ROUTE.

The various streams in the vicinity of Ithaca, both those flowing into the Cayuga Lake and those flowing south, present, therefore, scenes of extraordinary beauty. The many cascades and the gulf scenery attract a constantly increasing number of tourists, and for their accommodation conveniences of access to the more noted points have been made, so that the visitor is relieved of much of the fatigue usually attending the exploration of such places. Almost in the village itself, and within a few minutes' walk of the Ithaca Hotel, is Ithaca Fall, on Fall Creek. This stream flows through the grandest gorge in this magnificent region; there are eight falls on it within two miles of the village post-office, all surrounded by wonderful rock scenery. From the bridge on Aurora street one of the finest possible views is obtained of this cataract. The water leaps downward 150 feet at an angle of $70°$, and is broken into a multitude of cascades by the inequalities of rock surface over which it flows. Cascadilla Creek is another stream which finds its outlet through the village and whose picturesque scenery begins only a very short distance from the busiest portion of Ithaca. Six Mile Creek is also within easy walking distance from the Hotel and will well reward the lover of the picturesque for the fatigue of its exploration. Buttermilk Falls, Barnes's Glen, Lick Brook, Newfield Ravine, The West Branch, Enfield Ravine, Coy's Glen, Taghanic, McKinney's, Burdick's Glen, Salmon Creek, the Ludlowville Falls are all within ten miles of Ithaca, and are full of scenes of the most picturesque and extraordinary beauty, which will well reward the tourist for prolonging his stay in the vicinity. Ithaca is the seat of Cornell University, founded by the Hon. Ezra Cornell, and is also a place of extensive manufacturing industries. The Ithaca Organ and Piano Co. and the Calendar Clock Co. have very large factories here, employing many hands.

There is steamboat communication with all points on Cayuga Lake, and railroads connecting the town with the whole railroad system of the State.

THE ITHACA HOTEL, a large and well-kept house, affords excellent accommodations to the tourist who desires to spend a few days in the heart of this wonderful region.

PULPIT FALL—on Buttermilk Creek, Ithaca, N. Y.

ERIE RAILWAY ROUTE.

**TIOGA CENTRE, Tioga Co., N. Y.,**
*242 miles from New York. From Dunkirk, 218.*

A small station at the mouth of Catatunk Creek. Here are several mills and about sixty dwellings.

**SMITHBOROUGH, Tioga Co., N. Y.,**
*246 from New York. From Dunkirk, 214.*

A village in Tioga Township, containing about 300 inhabitants. The Southern Central R.R. has a depot here, and tri-weekly stages run to Nichols, N. Y., Windham, Herrick, Patterville, Camptown, and Orwell, Pa. A bridge crosses the Susquehanna here.

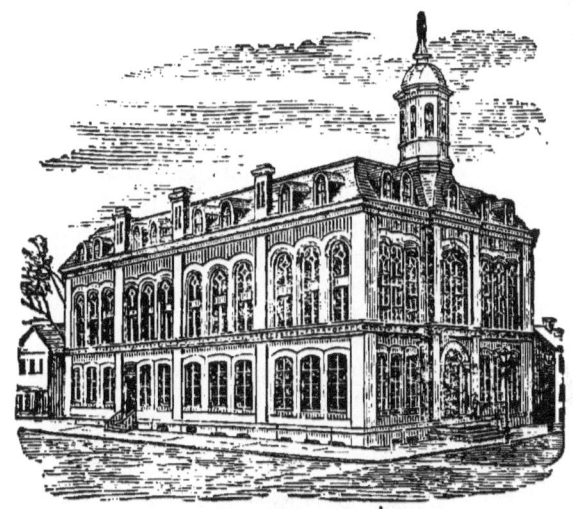

CORNELL LIBRARY, ITHACA, N. Y.

**BARTON, Tioga Co., N. Y.,**
*249 miles from New York. From Dunkirk, 211.*

This is a thriving and pretty situated village in the southeast corner of the township of the same name. The Susquehanna here bends towards the south and soon passes into Pennsylvania, across which it winds its way into Maryland, where it empties into the Chesapeake Bay. The railroad now crosses an intervale meadow and the Cayuta Creek on a high embankment and bridge, passing the village of Factoryville, which lies a little over a mile north of the railway.

ERIE RAILWAY ROUTE.

### WAVERLY, Tioga Co., N. Y.,
### 256 *miles from New York. From Dunkirk,* 204.

This is an incorporated village in the southwest part of Barton Township, very near the line of Pennsylvania, and near that of Chemung County. It has about 6,000 inhabitants, and is rapidly increasing. It contains an academy, five churches, and several manufactories. Near the station is Spanish Hill, the scene of an incident connected with the massacre of Wyoming. Three of the prisoners, who were being carried away by six Indians, rose in the night, and slaying five of their captors, escaped unharmed. Tioga Point, lying south of Waverly, is a tongue of land between the Susquehanna and Chemung rivers, which unite below it. It has some historical interest, as it was the rendezvous of the British and Indians before they ravaged the Wyoming Valley, and of the American forces under Sullivan and Clinton, in 1779, when in pursuit of Brandt after the massacre at Lackawaxen.

Waverly has superior railroad facilities. Besides the Erie, the Lehigh Valley, the Southern Central, and the Ithaca and Athens roads all have depots in the town. The Tioga Hotel, a new and spacious house, is the principal hotel in Waverly.

### CHEMUNG, Chemung Co., N. Y.,
### 260 *miles from New York. From Dunkirk,* 200.

This is the name of the railroad station and post-office. The little village is called Breckville.

### WELLSBURG, Chemung Co., N. Y.,
### 266 *miles from New York. From Dunkirk,* 194.

This is a manufacturing village in the southeast part of the township; population about 800. There are good hotels and three handsome churches. About two miles south of the village is a very picturesque glen, well worthy of a visit.

Stage connections are made tri-weekly for Centerville, Pennyville, Ridgeburg and Smithfield, Pa. There is a wire suspension bridge over the Chemung River at this place. In 1799 Gen. Sullivan and his army, on their march in pursuit of the British and Indians, encamped in this valley and threw up a breastwork. The enemy

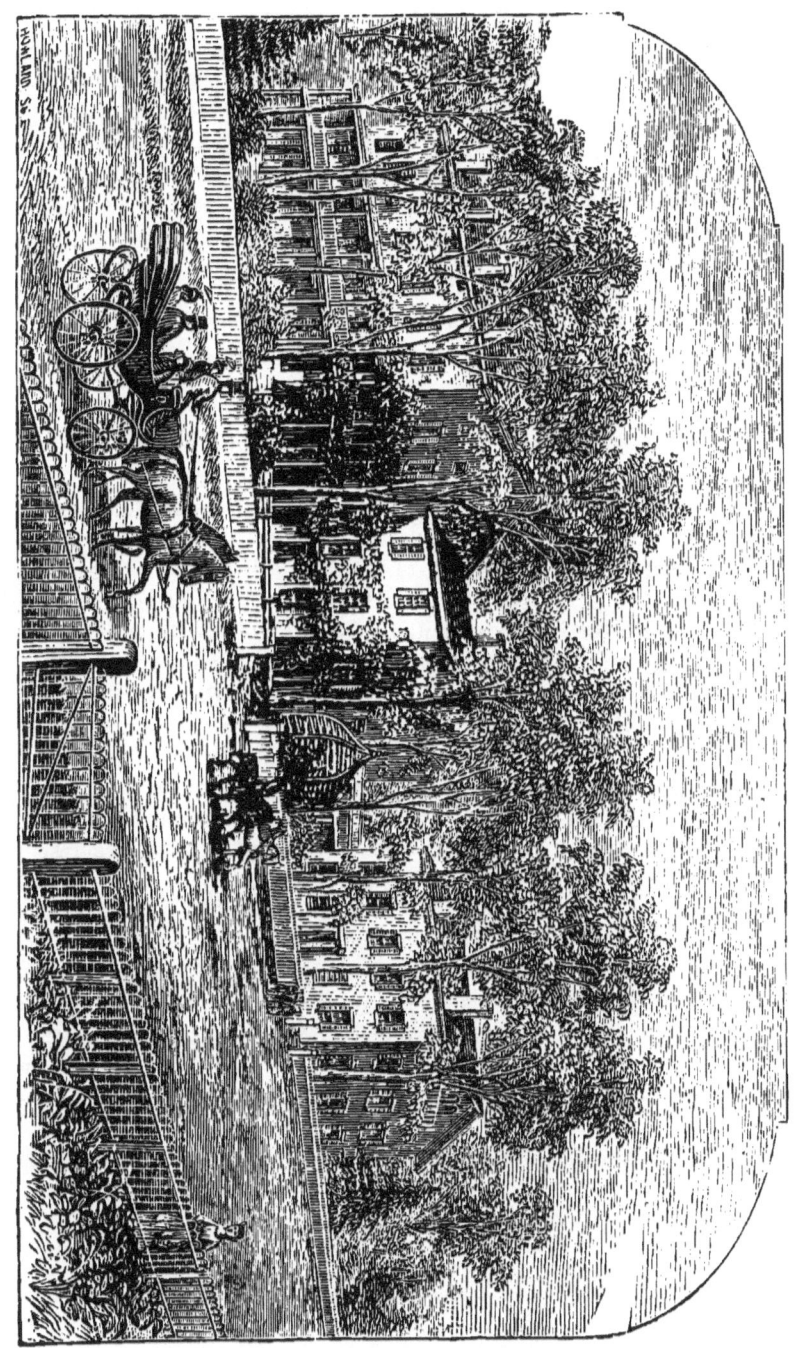

ELMIRA WATER-CURE.

## ERIE RAILWAY ROUTE.

were under command of Colonels Butler and Johnson and the notorious half-breed John Brandt. An encounter took place, August 29th, in which, after an obstinate conflict of two hours, the enemy were completely routed and dispersed. A monument marks the scene of this memorable struggle, having been erected on the centennial anniversary of the event.

### SOUTHPORT, Chemung, Co., N. Y.,
273 *miles from New York. From Dunkirk,* 187.
A station in the fifth ward of the city of Elmira.

### ELMIRA, Chemung Co., N. Y.,
274 *miles from New York. From Dunkirk,* 186.
HOTEL—FRASIER HOUSE, NEAR DEPOT.

This is one of those cities whose growth seems almost like magic, having grown up almost entirely within the last thirty years. It is, in fact, one of the contributions of the Erie Railway to the prosperity of the country. But a few years ago an insignificant village, it is now a city of over 20,000 inhabitants, with extensive manufactories and a large and growing trade. It is on the line of the Erie, the Northern Central, the Lehigh Valley R R., and the Utica, Ithaca, and Elmira R.R. The city is supplied with water from Seely and Cars Creeks, and Lake Eldridge. It has an efficient fire-department and police. The public schools of Elmira are among the best in the State. The school buildings are handsome and substantial, and are surrounded in every instance with play-grounds three to five acres in extent. There are about 3,000 children in attendance, with a good corps of teachers, and an efficient Board of Education. The Elmira Female College, under the care of the Synod of Geneva, is a large and amply endowed institution of learning. The Elmira Academy of Science, organized in 1861, has an astronomical observatory, in connection with the Female College, and a cabinet of geology. There are a number of literary and benevolent associations in Elmira, a State Reformatory, and a widely known water-cure establishment.

At Elmira the Erie Railway makes close connection with the Northern Central Railroad for Havana and Watkins Glens, the steamboats on Seneca Lake, and points beyond.

# FRASIER HOUSE,
### ELMIRA, N. Y.

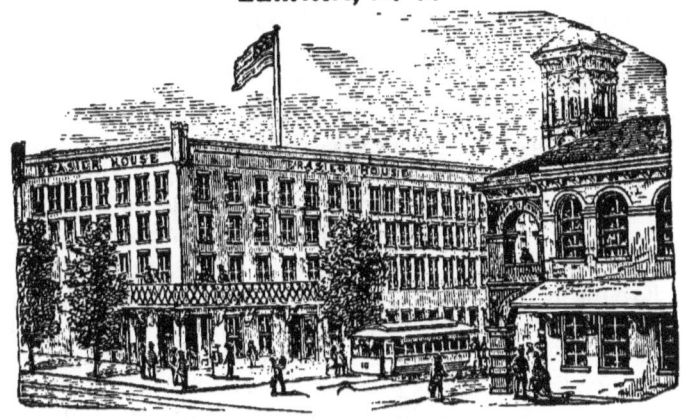

**A. J. DOBBINS, Proprietor.**

Thoroughly renovated and heated by steam.    Bells, baths, etc.
NO EXTRA CHARGE FOR STEAM.

**Near Union Depot.**      **TERMS, $2.00 PER DAY.**

---

Ask Your Dealer for

Gives a quick, brilliant, and durable polish, with positive nourishment to the leather. It is different in composition from common blackings, being based upon the French process with every valuable feature of the French style retained, while such improvements have been made as to insure a dryer and more durable gloss, with increased pliability of the leather.

# ERIE RAILWAY ROUTE,

## Watkins Glen.

Among the many places of beauty and interest accessible *via* the Erie Railway, none exceed in picturesque and romantic scenery the celebrated Watkins and Havana Glens. Watkins Glen is in close proximity to the village of Watkins, which is the county seat of Schuyler County, and has been made accessible to visitors by the construction of a series of rude staircases and bridges spanning the chasm at various points. The stream of water which here finds its way into Seneca Lake has, in the course of ages, cut its way through the mountain and formed a narrow and deep gorge, through which it runs, forming in its course a series of cascades, rapids and pools, which, taken with their weird surroundings, form a scene of almost indescribable beauty. Names have been given to various portions of the gorge, descriptive of the peculiar formation of each locality, such as Glen Cathedral, where the enclosing walls of rock widen into a vast amphitheater ; the Glen of Pools, where the action of the water has worn numerous basins in its rocky bed. The falls and cascades are also known by titles, such as "Entrance Cascade," "Minnehaha," "Sylvan Rapids," "Rainbow Falls," "The Artist's Dream," etc.

There are good hotels in Watkins for the accommodation of the immense number of visitors who assemble here every season. The Glen Mountain House is situated on Mount Watkins, in the glen. It is an excellent hotel, in every way first-class, and admirably adapted for accommodating summer visitors. The Glen Park Hotel, situated near the entrance to the glen, is the largest hotel in Watkins, and will accommodate 250 guests. It is a first-class house, has pleasant surroundings, and is open from June to November. The Lake View House is an excellent hotel, situated on high ground overlooking the village of Watkins and Seneca Lake. The house is supplied with all modern conveniences, and is under capable and efficient management. On the summit of Mount Watkins is an observatory, from which a view of unsurpassed beauty is obtained. At its foot lie the villages of Watkins and Havana, and a rural landscape charming to the eye. To the north, Seneca Lake stretches away to the blue hills, which merge almost imperceptibly into the azure of the sky. The walks and drives about Watkins are very attractive. The Fall Brook House, in the village, and nearest the railroad station, is an old-established and well-kept house. The charges are reasonable.

# SENECA LAKE
## STEAM NAVIGATION CO., Limited.

### TOURISTS POPULAR ROUTE
BETWEEN
### WATKINS GLEN,
**LONG POINT** (where are located the Long Point Hotel and Pavilion),

### GENEVA and NIAGARA FALLS.
SIX TRIPS DAILY DURING THE
### EXCURSION SEASON.

Close connections at GENEVA with N. Y. C. & H. R. and L. V. R. Rs., at WATKINS with N. C. Ry.

**MEALS ON STEAMERS.     FREE TRANSFER OF BAGGAGE.**

### W. B. DUNNING, Superintendent,
GENEVA, N. Y.

## ERIE RAILWAY ROUTE.

sonable, and the house, though not large, is well patronized. Stages run from the Fall Brook House to Tyrone and Ithaca daily, and triweekly to Monterey.

### HAVANA GLEN

is three miles south of Watkins. It is not so extensive as Watkins Glen, but has some views of wondrous beauty. The Bridal Veil Fall and the Curtain Cascade are perhaps among the most noted, but the tourist will find many others of almost equal beauty. The same methods of access have been adopted here as in Watkins Glen. There is a very striking difference in the character of the scenery in the two glens, and it would be hard to decide which is superior. In Watkins Glen the gorge is narrow, with jagged, uneven sides, alternately receding and approaching each other; the stream flows for a great part of its course in a very narrow channel, bursting here and there into rapids, cascades, and falls. Havana Glen is surrounded by walls square and even as the walls of a fortress; the current follows the peculiar lines of the strata, turning in its course at right angles, and carving out rectangular chambers and passage-ways with square corners and perpendicular sides. The stream is larger, the falls fewer, but more majestic, the pools not round, but square. Visitors should not fail to see both of the glens. The two make pictures whose wondrous beauty will linger in the memory forever.

### WEST JUNCTION, Chemung Co., N. Y.,

*278 miles from New York. From Dunkirk, 182.*

This station is one mile from the village of Horseheads, a thriving place of about 3,000 inhabitants. A stage runs to and from the village, connecting with all passenger trains. The greater part of the freight business of Horseheads is done at this station. There is a hotel at the junction, and in Horseheads there are two hotels, several churches, a large school-house, banks, etc.

### BIG FLATS, Chemung Co., N. Y.,

*284 miles from New York. From Dunkirk, 176.*

A small station in the township of the same name, near the line of Steuben County. Considerable quantities of tobacco are raised in this neighborhood.

# ST. DENIS HOTEL
### AND
# RESTAURANT,

Cor. Broadway and Eleventh Street,

### NEW YORK.

### THE MOST CENTRALLY LOCATED HOTEL IN THE CITY.

Being in the vicinity of all the leading Retail Stores and Principal Places of Amusement—of easy access from all the Depots and Ferries by Horse-Cars, Stage, or the Elevated Rail-Roads. Stages from Grand Central Depot pass the door.

ERIE RAILWAY ROUTE.

### CORNING, Steuben Co., N. Y.,
### 291 *miles from New York.* *From Dunkirk,* 169.

Corning is incorporated, and is one of the two county seats of Steuben County, Bath being the other. Its present name was given in 1852, in honor of Hon. Erastus Corning, of Albany. It is a large and rapidly growing place, and is pleasantly located. A high hill in its rear affords charming views of the surrounding scenery. The castellated building on the hill south of, and in sight from, the railway, is the State Arsenal. The Rochester division of the Erie Railway diverges from the main road here, and extends to Rochester. (For a description of this branch, see page 62.) The Corning and Blossburg Railway opens a communication to one of the finest beds of bituminous coal in Pennsylvania, which thus finds a ready market in Western New York. A disastrous fire destroyed a large portion of the business part of the place in 1850, but it was promptly rebuilt, and has since rapidly increased in size and importance. There is an extensive manufactory of glass, iron foundries, engine-building establishments, one of the finest public school buildings in the State. The DICKINSON HOUSE is the leading hotel.

### PAINTED POST, Steuben Co., N. Y.,
### 293 *miles from New York.* *From Dunkirk,* 167.

This is the oldest settlement in this part of the country, and derives its name from a monument said to have been erected in 1779, by the river-side, over the grave of the Indian chief Captain Montour, son of Queen Catharine. The monument erected by the companions of this brave and noted chieftain was a wooden post, upon which were painted various Indian devices. A painted wooden pole in the public square of the village preserves the tradition. There are two hotels, a public hall, bank, three churches, and a large mill for the manufacture of bark extract. Twenty million feet of lumber are manufactured here annually. The route of the Rochester Division, which has been running side by side with the main route from Corning, here diverges towards the north, following the valley of Conhocton River, while the main route, crossing the Conhocton near its junction with the Canisteo River, follows up the valley of the latter. These two rivers unite at Painted Post, forming the Chemung. Stages run daily to Monterey.

ITHACA FALL. N. Y.

ERIE RAILWAY ROUTE.

### ADDISON, Steuben Co., N. Y.,
*302 miles from New York. From Dunkirk, 158.*

An important and growing village in the township of the same name, on the north bank of the Canisteo River, at the junction of Tuscarora Creek. The original name given by the early settlers was Tuscarora; but it was changed to Addison, in honor of the English author of that name. It has six churches, a bank, and several mills and manufacturing establishments. There is an iron bridge over the Canisteo River at this place.

### RATHBONEVILLE, Steuben Co., N. Y.,
*307 miles from New York. From Dunkirk, 153.*

Has one church, a flouring-mill, two saw-mills, and forty dwellings. The adjacent country is hilly and rugged. Stages run to Hedgesville, N. Y., on Tuesdays and Fridays.

### CAMERON MILLS, Steuben Co., N.Y.,
*312 miles from New York. From Dunkirk, 148.*

A small village. Deer are found in the vicinity. There is a tri-weekly stage to Risingville, Merchantville, and Campbelltown.

### CAMERON, Steuben Co., N. Y.,
*315 miles from New York. From Dunkirk, 145.*

A village in a deep, wild valley, frequented by sportsmen, who hunt the deer in winter.

### ADRIAN, Steuben Co , N. Y.,
*323 miles from New York. From Dunkirk, 137.*

Formerly called Crosbyville ; contains one church and 30 dwellings.

### CANISTEO, Steuben Co., N. Y.,
*328 miles from New York. From Dunkirk, 132.*

An incorporated village on the south side of the river, nearly half a mile from the station. There are two hotels, two churches, a large academy, extensive chair and sash factories, a large tannery, and boot and shoe manufactory. Population 2,500. There is a tri-weekly stage to Rexville, N. Y., and a daily stage for Greenwood. The valley widens soon after leaving the station.

SAGE COLLEGE FOR WOMEN, Cornell University, Ithaca, N. Y.

ERIE RAILWAY ROUTE.

## HORNELLSVILLE, Steuben Co., N. Y.,
### 332 miles from New York. From Dunkirk, 128.
#### THE OSBORN IS THE LEADING HOTEL IN TOWN.

This place derives its name from the Hon. Geo. Hornell, the former proprietor of the township. It is situated at the junction of the Canisteo River and Caneadea Creek. The Canisteo River unites with the Tioga at Erwin, and with the Conhocton at Painted Post, and the combined streams form the Chemung River. There are an immense amount of side-tracks, ample engine-houses, repair-shops, and other railroad structures, as the village is the dividing-point of the Susquehanna and Western Divisions, and the point of junction of the Buffalo Division of the Erie Railway (for description of this branch, see p. 49). It has banks, newspapers, a flourishing library association, which maintains a course of popular lectures, and is one of the most efficient and attractive institutions of the kind in the interior of the State. There are churches of various denominations, and a population of about 9,000. The cars destined for Buffalo, Niagara Falls, etc., are here detached from those going west *via* Salamanca or Dunkirk. At the station is a spacious dining-saloon, where meals are served to travelers at regular hours. The road now leaves the valley of the Canisteo River, which it has been following up in a northwesterly direction, and bending around towards the south, up the Whitney valley, commences upon an ascending grade about fifty feet to a mile.

## ALMOND, Alleghany Co., N. Y.,
### 337 miles from New York. From Dunkirk, 123.

A manufacturing village of about 700 inhabitants, in the eastern part of the township of the same name. There are three churches, three flouring-mills, and several manufactories. A fine water-power is afforded by the Karr, McHenry, and Whitney Creeks, which, uniting here, form the Caneadea Creek.

## ALFRED, Alleghany Co., N. Y.,
### 341 miles from New York. From Dunkirk, 119.

The first-settled town in the county, contains a population of about 1,000. The place is also known as Baker's Bridge. Dairying is the principal business interest in the town, and the village has nine cheese-factories. There is a flourishing academy, two churches, several

## ERIE RAILWAY ROUTE.

mills, etc. A stage runs to Alfred Center three times daily. There are good hotels at Alfred and at Alfred Center. No liquor licenses are granted in this town. The location is healthy. Small game abound, and trout are found in the streams. Alfred University, under the control of the Sabbatharian, is located here.

### ANDOVER, Alleghany Co., N. Y.,
*350 miles from New York. From Dunkirk, 110.*

Has four churches, several mills, and 800 inhabitants. It is located on Dike Creek, a tributary of the Genesee River. The railway crosses the creek several times in descending its valley.

### WELLSVILLE, Alleghany Co., N. Y.,
*358 miles from New York. From Dunkirk, 102.*

This was formerly called the "Genesee Station," and is now an important and rapidly growing place, at the highest part of the Genesee valley reached by the railway. Dike's and Chenunda Creeks here unite with the Genesee River. This station has attained considerable importance within a year or two, owing to the discovery of petroleum in the immediate vicinity, and a few miles southward in Alleghany county, at Richburg and Bolivar. The Erie is connected with the new oil region by the Eldred and Cuba narrow-gauge railroad.

The trade of a large region of country, extending into Potter County, Pa., centers here, this being the nearest railway station, and accessible by the deep valleys of streams flowing into the Genesee. The route now changes abruptly to the north-west, following down the Genesee valley.

### SCIO, Alleghany Co., N. Y.,
*362 miles from New York. From Dunkirk, 98.*

Is a flourishing village of about 1,000 inhabitants. The country here is very uneven, the hills rising steep to a height of from 700 to 1,000 feet above the valleys.

### PHILLIPSVILLE, Alleghany Co., N. Y.,
*366 miles from New York. From Dunkirk, 94.*

The name of the village and post-office adjoining is Belmont. It is one of the county seats, and contains a court-house, jail, county clerk's office, etc. It is situated at the junction of Phillip's Creek with the Genesee River. The railway crosses to the west side of the river.

## ERIE RAILWAY ROUTE.

### BELVIDERE, Alleghany Co., N. Y.,
*370 miles from New York. From Dunkirk,* 90.

A village in the north-west part of Amity township, near the junction of Van Campen's Creek with the Genesee River, and about four miles above the mouth of Angelica Creek. It derives its name from the "Church" mansion, the first frame building erected in the county.

Stages run to Belfast, Oramel, and Caneadea daily, and to Angelica twice each day. Angelica, one of the shire towns of Alleghany County, is situated about two miles up this creek.

### FRIENDSHIP, Alleghany Co., N. Y.,
*374 miles from New York. From Dunkirk,* 86.

This village lies between the railway and the creek. It contains four churches, an academy, a musical university, and one of the finest public halls in Western New York. The principal business of the place is cheese and butter making. Stages connect daily for Nile, Richburg, and the oil regions, Bolivar, Little Genesee, and Ceres.

### CUBA, Alleghany Co., N. Y.,
*383 miles from New York. From Dunkirk,* 77.

This enterprising and flourishing village is near the west line of Alleghany County, and is increasing in importance owing to the Alleghany oil fields. It is connected with that region by the Eldred and Cuba Railroad, recently completed. The Tonawanda Valley and Cuba Railroad extends northward and joins the Buffalo Division of the Erie at Attica. Cattaraugus County, into which we pass next, s an elevated and uneven county, chiefly devoted to grazing in those ,ortions where the original timber has been removed.

### HINSDALE, Cattaraugus Co., N. Y.,
*390 miles from New York. From Dunkirk,* 70.

It is located at the junction of Ischua and Oil Creek. The route continues down Oil Creek, crossing it before it reaches its junction with the Alleghany. This is not the celebrated Oil Creek of Pennsylvania, where the great petroleum wells are found. It derives its name, however, from the so-called Seneca oil, which was formerly collected there by the Indians.

ERIE RAILWAY ROUTE.

### OLEAN, Cattaraugus Co., N. Y.,
395 *miles from New York. From Dunkirk*, 65.

At the junction of Oil Creek and the Alleghany River is an incorporated village of 5.000 inhabitants and is rapidly increasing in importance. Connection is made at this point with the Buffalo, New York, and Philadelphia R.R., and Olean, Bradford, and Warren R.R. Olean is one of the largest petroleum storing places in the world. The United Pipe Line Company has numerous iron tanks here, and it is from Olean that the crude petroleum is started on its journey to the seaboard through the iron pipes that carry it the entire distance. The business of the place is largely that of refining, shipping, and dealing in petroleum. There are upwards of 300 oil tanks here and an Oil Exchange.

### ALLEGHANY, Cattaraugus Co., N. Y.,
399 *miles from New York. From Dunkirk*, 61.

A prosperous village with about 1,500 inhabitants. A Franciscan College and Convent are located in the vicinity, and St. Elizabeth's Academy, under the charge of the Sisters of the Order of St. Francis. Four miles from this station we come into the Indian Reservation, which lies along the river and extends from the Pennsylvania line 25 miles in a north-east direction, comprising 42 square miles of the finest agricultural region in the country.

### VANDALIA, Cattaraugus Co., N. Y.,
404 *miles from New York. From Dunkirk*, 56.

A hamlet on the east line of Carrolton Township. The Vandalia Chemical Works are situated here.

### CARROLTON, Cattaraugus Co., N. Y.,
408 *miles from New York. From Dunkirk*, 52.

This is the junction of the Bradford Branch Railway, extending up the valley of the Tunegawant Creek to the extensive oil fields of McKean Co., Pa. (see p. 80). The country in the vicinity of Carrolton is wild, and deer, small game, and trout abound.

### GREAT VALLEY, Cattaraugus Co, N. Y.,
411 *miles from New York. From Dunkirk*, 49.

The post-office is Kill Buck, the population about 1,600. There are two hotels, several churches, and a commodious school building.

ERIE RAILWAY ROUTE.

The principal business of the place is the manufacture of lumber, shooks, hubs, and spokes. The famous Rock City is about 4 miles distant. The streams in the vicinity abound with trout and other fish. Stage connection daily with Peth and Ellicottville.

**SALAMANCA, Cattaraugus Co., N. Y.,**
415 *miles from New York. From Dunkirk*, 45. *Population*, 3,000.
Situated at the junction of the Little Valley Creek with the Alleghany River. It is the initial point of the New York, Penn., and Ohio Railway, extending through Pennsylvania and Ohio to Cincinnati and Cleveland (see p. 76). The railway company have here repair-shops, and there is an extensive tannery and lumbering establishment. Much of the surrounding country is still forest, and lumbering forms the leading pursuit.

**LITTLE VALLEY, Cattaraugus Co., N. Y.,**
421 *miles from New York. From Dunkirk*, 39. *Population*, 700.
The county seat was removed from Ellicottville to Little Valley, and the first courts held at the latter place in June, 1868. The court house is of brick, 56x82 feet, with slate roof, and the record offices therein are fireproof. The jail is a separate brick building adjacent, and both are supplied with spring water from a source 1½ mile distant. The Cattaraugus County Fair Grounds are located here. They contain 25 acres of land with suitable buildings, and are handsomely laid out. In this township occurs a singular formation known as Rock City. It is situated upon the summit of a hill 400 feet above the valley, and 2,000 feet above tidewater. The rock, consisting of conglomerate, is arranged in regular blocks, with sharp angles and perpendicular sides, presenting the appearance of courtyards, or squares, in the midst of numerusos treets and alleys. "The large trees which stand upon the top of the immense blocks have often sent their roots down the sides, where they are sustained by the deep soil, supporting the huge growth above upon an almost barren rock. The blocks are from 30 to 35 feet in thickness, and, standing regularly arranged, present an imposing appearance." This strange freak of Nature attracts hundreds of visitors annually. There are three hotels and three churches; the manufacture of butter and cheese is the leading industry. Stages run daily to Napoli, East Napoli, and Randolph, on the A. and G. W. R.R.

ERIE RAILWAY ROUTE.

### CATTARAUGUS, Cattaraugus Co., N. Y.,
*428 miles from New York. From Dunkirk, 32.*

An important village on the side hill forming the west slope of the valley of the south branch of Cattaraugus Creek.

### DAYTON, Cattaraugus Co., N. Y.,
*438 miles from New York. From Dunkirk, 22.*

This station is 1,595 feet above the level of the sea, and 1,015 above the lake at Dunkirk. From here the grade descends all the way to the lake. The Buffalo and Southwestern Division connects here, giving communication with Gowanda and Buffalo on the north, and Jamestown and Chautauqua Lake on the south. The best-appointed cheese factory in the county is located at this place.

### PERRYSBURG, Cattaraugus Co., N. Y.,
*441 miles from New York. From Dunkirk, 19.*

Quite a large manufacturing business is carried on here. Versailles, five miles north, and Gowanda, four miles east, are important villages. Stage daily for Gowanda, and for Versailles.

### SMITH'S MILLS, Chautauqua Co., N. Y.,
*448 miles from New York. From Dunkirk, 12.*

### FORESTVILLE, Chautauqua Co., N. Y.,
*452 miles from New York. From Dunkirk, 8.*

Is a place of considerable importance. It contains a population of about 1,200, several mills, and manufactories, a free academy, etc.

### DUNKIRK, Chautauqua Co., N. Y.,
*460 miles from New York. Population, 7,000.*

Was incorporated in 1837. Its present charter was granted in 1867. It is a lake port, and the west terminus of the original line of the Erie Railway. The harbor is entirely artificial, being formed by piers and a breakwater. Extensive wharves and warehouses have been built for a large commerce. There is a large locomotive manufactory, an extensive foundry and machine shop, planing-mills, and a large trade in lumber. The village is regularly laid out, and a street railroad connects it with Fredonia. At Dunkirk, connection is made with the Lake Shore and Michigan Southern Railway for all points South and West.

VIEW OF CHAUTAUQUA, N. Y.—SEAT OF NATIONAL SUNDAY SCHOOL ASSEMBLY.

# CHAUTAUQUA ASSEMBLY.

LEWIS MILLER, Akron, Ohio, *Pres't.*
A. K. WARREN, Mayville, N. Y., *Sec'y.*
E. A. SKINNER, Westfield, N. Y., *Treas'r.*
J. H. VINCENT, D. D., Plainfield, N. J., *Supt. of Instruction.*

F. H. ROOT, Buffalo, N. Y. } *Vice-*
JACOB MILLER, Canton, Ohio. } *Pres'ts*
F. D. CARLEY, Louisville, Ky. }

A. K. WARREN, Mayville N. Y., *Supt. of Grounds*

### EXECUTIVE COMMITTEE.
H. A. MASSEY, Cleveland, Ohio.
JACOB MILLER, Canton, Ohio.
H. A. PRATT, Chautauqua, N. Y.
J. C. GIFFORD, Westfield, N. Y.
WM. THOMAS, Meadville, Pa.

The now famous Chautauqua Assembly and Summer School is located at Chautauqua Lake in Western New York. It was organized in 1874, and holds annual meeting in July and August. It is a vast educational, religious and recreative institution, to which tens of thousands resort every season; the "*Original*" of all the modern "*Assemblies,*" and a centre of intellectual and religious influence.

Chautauqua is nine miles south from Lake Erie and seven hundred and fifty (750) feet above it. It is midway between New York and Chicago, three hours ride by rail from Buffalo, five hours from Cleveland, nine hours from Pittsburg, fourteen hours from Cincinnati, sixteen from Philadelphia, thirteen hours from Saratoga and Round Lake, eighteen from New York, nineteen from Baltimore, twenty from Washington, twenty-one from Chicago, and twenty-two hours from St. Louis.

Its elevation is fourteen hundred (1,400) feet above the ocean, "the place where the perfection of water scenery and the purity of mountain air is found," with freedom from summer pests, such as mosquitoes, etc.

The meetings at Chautauqua include the Annual Sessions of "The Chautauqua Teachers' Retreat," "The Chautauqua School of Languages," "The Foreign Missionary Institute," "The Chautauqua Musical College," "The Chautauqua School of Theology," the annual session of "The Chautauqua Sunday School Assembly," and the various meetings connected with "The Chautauqua Literary and Scientific Circle," "The Look-up Legion," and the new "Chautauqua Young Folk's Reading Union."

Lectures, Concerts, Class Drills, Organ Concerts, Stereoptican Exhibitions, "The Athenian Watch Fires," Fire-works, Illuminated fountains, etc., etc., will g've variety, instruction and entertainment.

The Association has erected, at great expense, many fine Public Buildings, among them a mammoth Amphitheater which as an audience room is grand and complete. In lighting their beautiful forests and public buildings with the Brush Electric Light the Association is, as heretofore, in advance in having the best of everything.

Among the attractions for 1883, are "The Beautiful Fountains," illuminated by the "Electric Light;" "The Illuminated Fleet;" the "C. L. S. C. Camp Fire;" "The Class Vigil;" the second "Commencement of the C. L. S. C.;" "The Children's Bonfire;" "The Organ Concerts;" "The Art and Archæological Museum;" "The Chautauqua School of Theology;" "The Musical College;" "Elementary Singing Schools;" and the "Musical Reading Circle."

Boarding may be had at reasonable rates. Fine cottages can be rented for the season entire or by rooms, also tents of all sizes.

The Lake is about 20 miles in length, and steamboats, "first-class," pass over it almost hourly, touching at all points and connecting at either end with the different railroads. The leading railroads issue excursion tickets at about half rates.

There are upon the grounds offices of the American Express Company and Western Union Telegraph Company, and Telephone connections with Mayville, Westfield and Jamestown. There is also a government post-office with four daily mails.

### THE HOTEL ATHENÆUM.

Has been enlarged and completed, and will be continued under the management of Billy Lewis, of Florida. It has elegant and capacious rooms, broad verandahs fronting the Lake, with a dining-room capacity of six hundred sittings. Five hundred guests can be accommodated at the Athenæum. The arrangements, internal and external, are complete, and the management is first class.

For information concerning the department of instruction, including the "C. L. S. C." address Dr. J. H. Vincent, Plainfield, N. J.

For all other information, such as concerning routes, rents, accommodations, etc., etc., address A. K. Warren, Secretary, Mayville, N. Y.

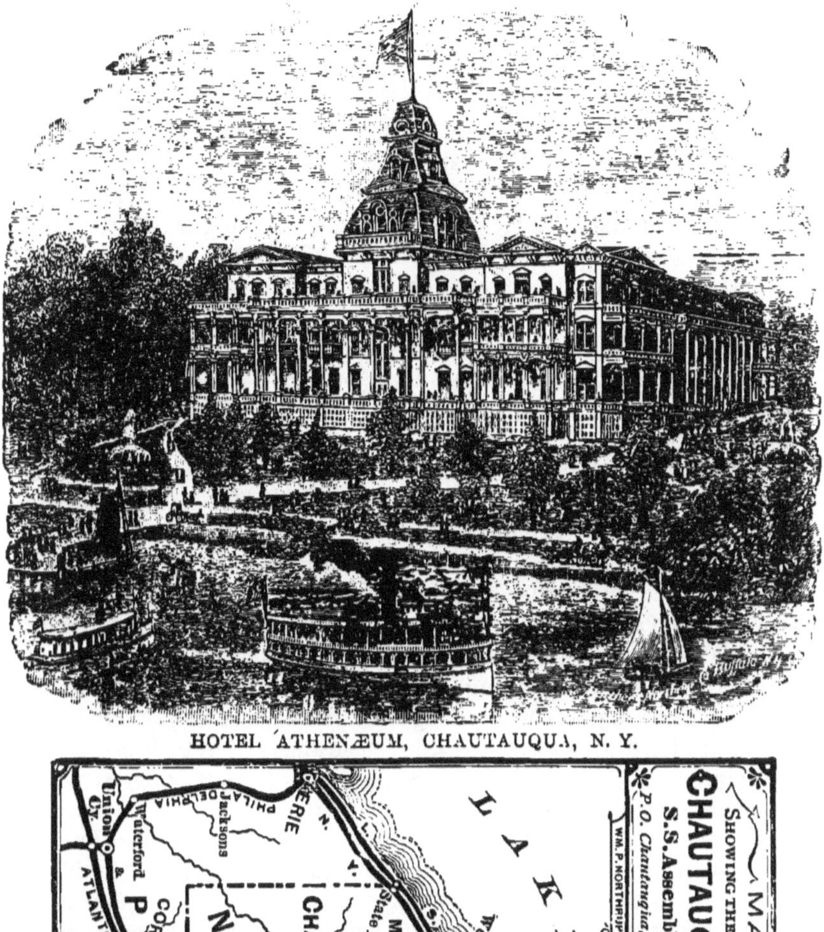

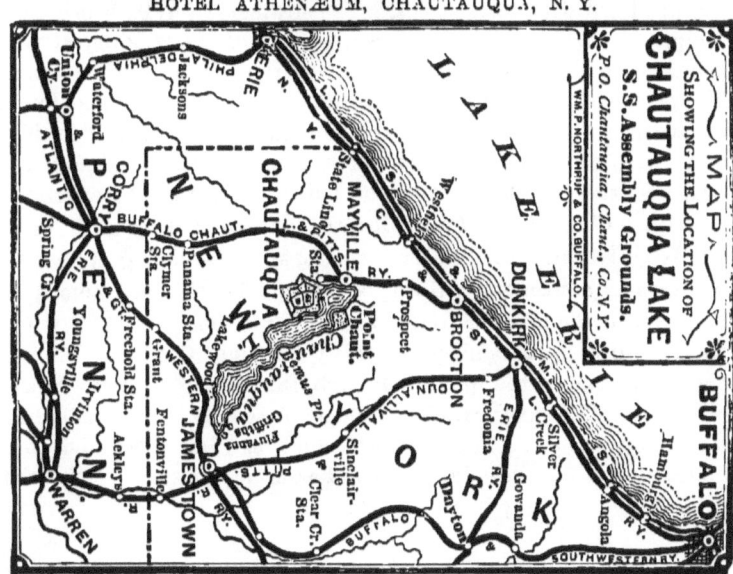

HOTEL ATHENÆUM, CHAUTAUQUA, N. Y.

ERIE RAILWAY ROUTE.

# CHAUTAUQUA LAKE.

Chautauqua Lake lies in the center of Chautauqua county, the westernmost county of the State New York. It is 1,400 feet above the sea, and 723 feet above Lake Erie, which is only eight miles away. Chautauqua Ridge, near Mayville, is the great water-shed which divides the waters of Lake Erie from those of the the Alleghany river. On one side, the waters flow to the Atlantic through the lakes and the St. Lawrence; and on the other they find their way to the Gulf of Mexico. Nearly on this summit is Chautauqua Lake, twenty miles in length, with a depth of about ninety-five feet in the deepest part. It is fed by natural springs. The head of the lake is at Mayville, and the outlet through Conewango Creek, which flows through Jamestown.

But little is known of the early history of Chautauqua Lake. The Indians named it Juduqua (diadem of beauty). The diary of Father Bonnecamps, who accompanied the French explorer De Celoron from Lachine, Canada, to the Ohio, contains perhaps the only authentic account of its discovery by white men, on July 23, 1749. The French called it "Chatacouin." Steamboats have traversed its waters from Jamestown to Mayville since 1828. Jamestown is reached from the lake, through a winding outlet, about three miles in length. It is scarcely wide enough for steamboats to pass, and the banks are lined with forest trees. The steamers literally brush along among the boughs at times, and remind one of the winding streams of Florida, of the Ocklawaha and the luxuriant lagoons of the South.

The principal points of interest are Mayville at the north, and Jamestown at the south end of the lake; Point Chautauqua, Maple Springs, Bay View, Long Point, Bemus's Point, Griffith's Point and Fluvanna on the east shore. Chautauqua and Lakewood are on the west shore (see map). Chautauqua, Point Chautauqua, and Lakewood have the most extensive and best accommodations, each having special advantages and attractions. Good board may be obtained among the farmers about the lake for from $5 to $8 per week.

CHAUTAUQUA is the name of the "Assembly Grounds," brought prominently before the public through Dr. Vincent's grand conception of the National Sunday School Assembly, the Chautauqua Literary Circle, etc. The original name of Fair Point has been abandoned. This place has a world-wide reputation. More than

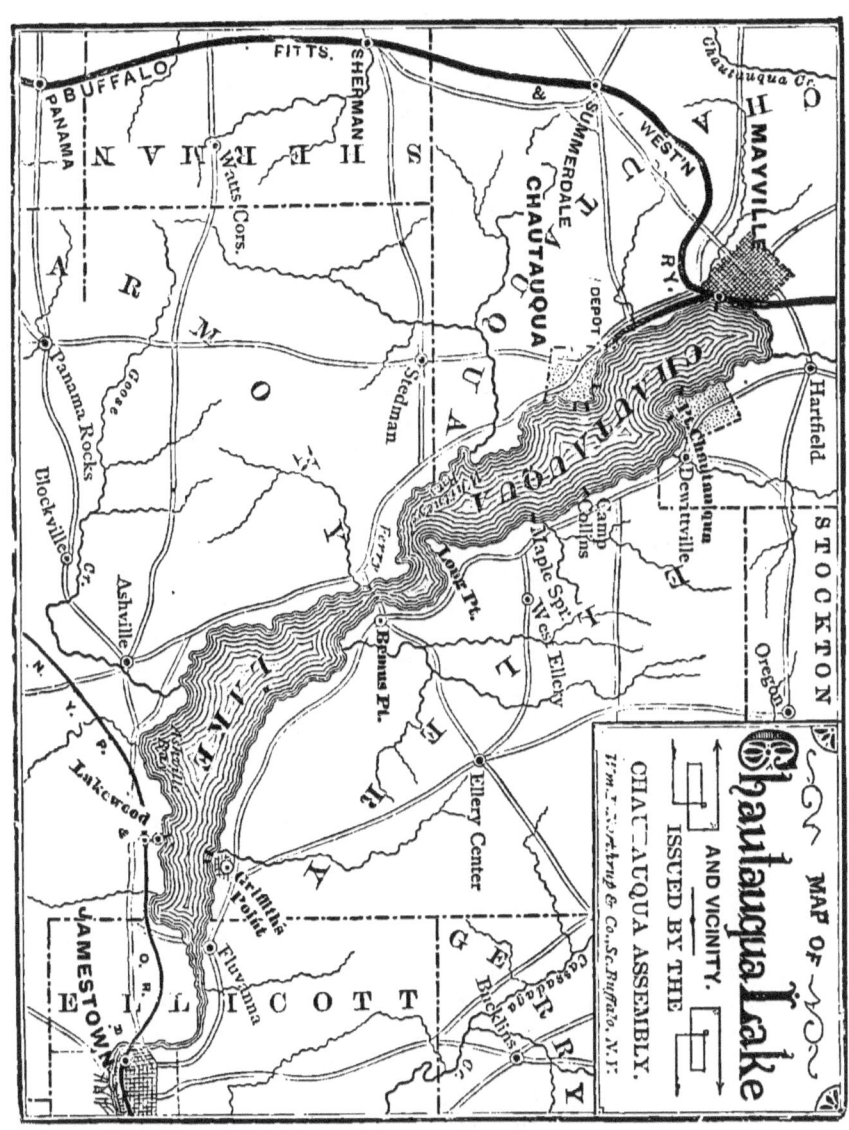

100,000 people visit it annually, and still it grows as its grand objects become understood. Here also is held the "Summer school in the woods," known as the Chautauqua Literary Circle, with branches throughout the country for special reading and self-improvement. The Chautauqua meetings are under the direction of a Board, and the work is divided into six departments, namely: 1. School of Languages; 2. Teachers' Retreat; 3. Foreign Missionary Institute; 4. Sunday School Assembly; 5. Literary and Scientific Circle; 6. Young Folks' Reading Union. Dr. J. H. Vincent is the Superintendent of instruction in all of these. The "Chautauqua idea" has become very popular within a few years. The Chautauqua Association numbers its tens of thousands in every part of the country. It not only brings the people together for a summer rest, but it also affords a school in almost every department of learning, and under the guidance of good instructors. The association owns about 80 acres of ground, most of which is covered with a native forest, in which are situated the great tabernacle and other buildings for holding meetings, the Hotel Athenæum and some 300 handsome cottages.

POINT CHAUTAUQUA, situated nearly opposite Mayville and Chautauqua, and is on the east side of the lake. It occupies the highest ground on the lake, and the piazzas of the Grand Hotel command a very fine view of the lake. The Point Chautauqua grounds, 100 acres, are owned by a Stock Company, and controlled by a Board of Managers, two-thirds of whom are Baptists. The aim of the Association is to provide a pleasant summer resort, free from all demoralizing influences. This feature should be borne in mind, because so many people have the impression that Chautauqua and Point Chautauqua are mere camp-grounds. They are more properly "Associations," formed by Methodists and Baptists mostly, for the purpose of bringing together a congenial class of people, with a community of interest in building up a summer resort combining health, culture, and comfort with religious exercises. Other denominations will find a hearty welcome at both of the above-named places.

LAKEWOOD, formerly Lake View, is the Chautauqua Lake station of the N. Y. P. and O. (formerly Atlantic and Great Western) Railroad. Quite a little settlement has sprung up here, owing to the influx of summer visitors. There are two excellent hotels here. The Kent House has four floors, with wide piazzas around each, and it fronts 500 feet on the lake with a dining-room 175 feet long. The Lake View House is admirably situated in a natural grove. It has wide verandas with charming views. This house contains a large assembly-room, with a glass front toward the lake, where promenading and dancing are in order. Both hotels have all the modern conveniences, and the prices are very reasonable.

Chautauqua Lake is most easily accessible from New York and all points East by the Erie Railway to Jamestown or Lakewood; from Buffalo to Jamestown over the Buffalo and Southwestern division of the Erie; or from Chicago, Cleveland, Cincinnati, and points West, by lines connecting with the New York, Pennsylvania and Ohio Railroad, which run direct to the shores of the Lake. A number of fine steamers afford quick and cheap transportation between all points of interest along the Lake. Of these the largest and best are those of the PEOPLE'S LINE, which run in connection with trains of Erie and N. Y., P. & O. Railways.

## SHERMAN HOUSE,
A. M. SHERMAN, Proprietor.  JAMESTOWN, N. Y.

175 Rooms in Suites. Every Room Heated with Steam. Elevator, Hot and Cold Water.

POINT CHAUTAUQUA, CHAUTAUQUA LAKE, N. Y.

ERIE RAILWAY ROUTE.

## BUFFALO DIVISION OF THE ERIE RAILWAY.
### FROM HORNELLSVILLE TO BUFFALO.

**HORNELLSVILLE, Steuben Co., N. Y.,**
332 *miles from New York. From Buffalo*, 91.
This is the terminus of the Susquehanna Division, and point of junction of the Buffalo Division with the main line of the Erie Railway. The cars destined for Buffalo, Niagara Falls, etc., are here detached from those going west *via* Salamanca or Dunkirk (for description of Hornellsville, see page 43).

**ARKPORT, Steuben Co., N. Y.,**
337 *miles from New York. From Buffalo*, 86.
A small village whose chief business is in lumber.

**BURNS, Alleghany Co., N. Y.,**
340 *miles from New York. From Buffalo*, 83.
Every train on the road stops at this station. A large business is done in shipping produce, especially potatoes, of which immense quantities are annually sent to market. The place is remarkably healthy.

**CANASERAGA, Alleghany Co., N. Y.,**
344 *miles from New York. From Buffalo*, 79.
In the northern part of the township, and contains an academy under Baptist management, a graded school, several mills, and about 900 inhabitants. It is a thriving village. There is a daily stage to Dansville.

**GARWOODS, Alleghany Co., N. Y.,**
347 *miles from New York. From Buffalo*, 76.
A small station.

**SWAINVILLE, Alleghany Co., N. Y.,**
349 *miles from New York. From Buffalo*, 74.
A post village on the line of Livingston County. The manufacture of lumber and barrels is the principal industry.

The surface of this section is a hilly upland, divided into several distinct ridges. Near the village is Chautauqua Valley, a romantic defile. The streams are tributaries of the Canaseraga and Black Creek, and afford a number of good sites for water-power, some of which have been improved.

ERIE RAILWAY ROUTE.

### DALTON, Livingston Co., N. Y.
*356 miles from New York. From Buffalo, 67.*

This station was formerly called Nunda. The village of Nunda is situated on the Genesee Valley Canal, about three miles north of the station. It has two good hotels, two grist-mills, a tannery, two newspapers, two banks, saw-mills, a furnace, machine-shop, cheese factory, carriage factory, a steam cabinetware factory, an academy, and six churches. Stages run to and from the station, connecting with all passenger trains, and connect twice daily with stage from Mount Morris. Population about 1,500. At the station is a thriving village of about seventy dwelling-houses, a church, twelve or fifteen places of business, and a new hotel with good accommodations.

### HUNT'S HOLLOW, Livingston Co., N. Y.,
*358 miles from New York. From Buffalo, 65.*

A small post village, containing two churches, a tannery, and about thirty houses. Two miles north of the station is the village of Oakland, a hamlet containing two churches, a grist and saw mill, a woolen factory, tannery, furnace, and thirty-five or forty dwellings.

### PORTAGE, Livingston Co., N. Y.,
*362 miles from New York. From Buffalo, 61.*

Portage is a village of 1,519 inhabitants, located on the Genesee Valley Canal, and the Genesee River. In its immediate vicinity are the celebrated PORTAGE FALLS, of the Genesee River Falls, three in number, each of which is remarkable for its beauty and grandeur. The Upper or Horseshoe Falls, seventy feet high, are about three-quarters of a mile below the village. The Middle Falls are about one-quarter of a mile farther down the river. Here the water pours in an unbroken sheet into a chasm 110 feet below, which is bounded by perpendicular ledges. A cave, called the "Devil's Oven," has been worn into the rocks on the west bank, near the bottom of the falls. In low water 100 persons can be seated in it, but when the river is high it is filled with water. Two miles below the Middle Falls, before reaching the third, the river pursues a winding course between perpendicular walls, across which a man might almost leap, then descends in a succession of rocky steps almost as regular as a staircase, dives under a shelving rock, and descends into a narrow

PORTAGE FALLS AND BRIDGE, PORTAGEVILLE, N. Y.

pass about fifteen feet wide. Descending perpendicularly for twenty feet, it strikes against the base of high rocks, whirls back, and, turning nearly at right angles, falls into a deep pool overhung with shelving rocks. "Sugar Loaf," an isolated mass of rock fifteen feet in diameter and 100 feet high, rises from the river-bed at a bend in its course, and receives nearly the whole force of the rushing waters. These falls are accessible only from the west side. The perpendicular bank on the west of the river is 380 feet high at one point. The old bridge by which the railway crossed the river was the largest wooden railroad bridge in the world. This bridge was built at a cost of $175,000, and stood upon thirteen strong stone piers set in the bed of the river, and rising sufficiently above high-water mark to be secure against freshets. Above these piers a timber trestlework rose 234 feet, on the top of which the track of the road was laid. The bridge was 800 feet long, and so constructed that any timber in the whole structure could be removed and replaced at pleasure. This splendid structure was destroyed by fire on the night of May 5th, 1875, and has been replaced by a fine iron bridge, constructed by the Watson Manufacturing Co., of Paterson, N. J. The dimensions correspond to those of the old wooden structure above described. The first and second falls can be seen from the bridge, and present a grand appearance as they are seen in the distance dashing over the rocks and plunging into the black basin. In some places the rocks of the ravine are 300 feet high, and small streams, trickling over the top of this wall, dissolve into blue mist long before they reach the bottom. The Genesee Valley Canal crosses the river on an aqueduct just above the bridge, then, running parallel with the river, passes under the railroad bridge on the high bluff of rocks forming the east bank of the river. The perforations for a tunnel, which was commenced and then abandoned, may be seen in driving from the hotel to the bottom of the ravine. Altogether, this place will well repay the visitor who has sufficient leisure for a stay of some days. The first settlement in this part of the country was made in 1804, along the banks of the river in this immediate neighborhood. Portageville, the nearest village, is on the west side of the river, a little south of the station, in the township of Genesee Falls, Wyoming County, the river here forming the boundary between the two counties. It has five churches and several mills. There is a large and good hotel near he station, and another

LITTLE GLEN IRIS FALLS—PORTAGE, N. Y.

in Portageville. There is a daily stage for Hiscox, Fillmore, Hume, and Oramel, connecting at Oramel with stage for Belvidere.

**CASTILE, Wyoming Co., N. Y.,**
*366 miles from New York. From Buffalo, 57.*

A village of 1,500 inhabitants, situated on Wolf Creek and the Genesee River, in the southwestern part of the township. There are four churches and a music hall. There is a water-cure establishment, two hotels, a foundry, carriage factory, marble works, etc.

There is a stage for East Pike and Pike daily.

**GAINESVILLE, Wyoming Co., N. Y.,**
*368 miles from New York. From Buffalo, 55.*

At this station connection is made with the Rochester and Pine Creek Railway, running to SILVER LAKE and PERRY, a distance of six miles. Silver Lake is a charming little sheet of water, and is much frequented as a summer resort. There is a good hotel, and the surrounding scenery is quite attractive. Perry is a thriving village near the outlet of the lake.

**WARSAW, Wyoming Co., N. Y.,**
*375 miles from New York. From Buffalo, 48.*

This is the county seat of Wyoming County. The village is about a mile east of the station on Oatka Creek. It contains the county buildings, several churches, various manufacturing establishments, and an acadamy. Recently this entire region has come into great prominence by the discovery of the richest deposits of salt ever found. Development of the new industry of salt manufacture is rapid.

Stages run daily to Arcade, in the south-western corner of the county, twenty-five miles, and to Batavia, the county-seat of Genesee County. On the Arcade stage route is WETHERSFIELD SPRINGS, six miles from Warsaw, a place of some importance, and the seat of the " Doolittle Institute," founded and endowed by Ormus Doolittle, Esq.

**DALE, Wyoming Co., N. Y.**
*381 miles from New York. From Buffalo, 42.*

A small post village.

**LINDEN, Genesee Co., N. Y.**
*385 miles from New York. From Buffalo, 38.*

This village is located in the southern part of the township and county; it contains a flouring and saw mill, a furnace and about

## ERIE RAILWAY ROUTE.

sixty dwellings. The surrounding country is noted for its production of apples.

### ATTICA, Wyoming Co., N. Y.,
*392 miles from New York. From Buffalo, 31.*

Is in the north-western part of the township, on Tonawanda Creek; was incorporated in 1837. It has a flourishing Union school, a bank, a newspaper office, a flouring-mill, five churches. The Rochester Division of the Erie Railway, which diverges from the main line at Corning, and passes through Avon and Batavia, here reunites with the North-western Division, forming a single line from this point to Buffalo. A branch of the N. Y. C. and H. R.R. extends from here to Batavia. There are stage connections daily for Varysburg, Johnsonburg, East Java, Java Village, North Java, and Sheldon.

### GRISWOLD, Genesee Co., N. Y.,
*395 miles from New York. From Buffalo, 28.*

A small station.

### DARIEN, Genesee Co., N. Y.,
*398 miles from New York. From Buffalo, 25.*

Darien Center and Darien City are two villages of Darien township, and lie about two miles apart, and half a mile north of the railway.

### ALDEN, Erie Co., N. Y.,
*404 miles from New York. From Buffalo, 19.*

Contains two churches, two hotels, and a steam tannery. Taylor Park, a handsome grove containing 30 acres, has been fitted for excursion parties, and a branch track connects it with the Erie R.R. Stages connect twice daily for Franklin Springs and Cowlesville.

### TOWN LINE, Erie Co., N. Y.,
*409 miles from New York. From Buffalo, 14.*

The post village of this name is about a mile south of the station, and is partly in Darien township.

### LANCASTER, Erie Co., N. Y.,
*413 miles from New York. From Buffalo, 10.*

An incorporated village in the western part of the township. It is also a station on the N. Y. C. and H. R.R.

ERIE RAILWAY ROUTE.

**CHEEKTOWAGA, Erie Co., N. Y.,**
*415 miles from New York. From Buffalo, 8.*
The route in its approach to Buffalo converges quite near to the New York Central Railway. The Indian name of this place, of which the present is a corruption, was "Jiik-do-waah-geh," and signified "the place of the crab-apple tree." There are two hotels with fair accommodations. Springs of sulphur water have been discovered in the township.

**EAST BUFFALO, Erie Co., N. Y.,**
*421 miles from New York. From Buffalo, 2.*
Is within the city of Buffalo, and is the point where the Niagara Falls Branch of the Erie Railway intersects the main line.

**BUFFALO, Erie Co., N. Y.,**
*423 miles from New York.*
Buffalo is situated at the eastern extremity of Lake Erie, and extends nearly ten miles along the Lake Shore and the Niagara River, covering an area of about forty square miles. It is the western terminus of the Erie Canal, and has a perfect net-work of railroads radiating from it to every point in the United States. Besides the Erie Railway, there are the New York Central and Hudson River Railroad, the Grand Trunk, the Lake Shore and Michigan Southern the Canada Southern, the Great Western, the Buffalo, New York and Philadelphia, and the Buffalo and Jamestown Railroads. From its position, therefore, Buffalo is at once the natural key to the commerce of the Great Lakes and the Great North-west, and also the artificial gate through which the boundless grain-fields of the West pour their treasures into Eastern markets. Next to New York city Buffalo is the most important commercial city in the State. The French, who were its first visitors, named it "Buffle"—English, Buffalo—from the wild oxen which they saw in great droves around. In 1813, during the war with Great Britain, this place suffered greatly; every house was destroyed but one, which is still standing near the corner of Mohawk and Main streets. In 1815 buildings were again erected, and in 1825 Congress voted $80,000 for the sufferers. The principal influence in producing the rapid growth of the city was exerted by the construction of the Erie Canal, completed in October, 1825, which has its western terminus here. From

## ERIE RAILWAY ROUTE.

the time when the quarrel between Buffalo and Black Rock, as to which should have the terminus, was decided in favor of Buffalo, to the present, it has been rapidly increasing in size and importance. Soon after this first period it was not unusual in summer to see the plains of Buffalo white with the tents of emigrants, who, unable to obtain better accommodation in the crowded city, there awaited the arrival of the steamboats, which were to convey them across the lakes to their new homes. The harbor of Buffalo, formed by the Great Buffalo Creek, was, before the construction of the Erie Canal, obstructed by the washing in of sand from the lake, but by the energy and enterprise of the citizens a pier or breakwater was, after several failures, extended so far out into the lake as to control its "wash," and to enable the spring freshets in the creek to scour out the deposits and maintain a deep and lasting channel. It was this success that decided the location at this place of the canal terminus. A continuous line of wharves extends along Buffalo Creek. The Erie basin, just north of Buffalo Creek, is protected by a breakwater from the lake storms, and the Ohio basin, a little more than a mile up the creek, contains ten acres of sufficient depth to float the largest lake vessels. The Black Rock Ship-canal extends more than a mile between Buffalo Creek and the lake, and is connected with the creek, the basins, and the Erie Canal by numerous slips. At the end of the pier, which extends 1,500 feet into the lake, is a lighthouse, strongly built of stone and iron, and furnished with a first-class Fresnel dioptric light. The site of the city rises gradually, and in one or two places attains a height of 100 feet, but the greater portion of its area occupies an extended plain, averaging fifty feet above the lake. The more elevated portions afford fine views of the city, Niagara River, Lake Erie, and the Canada shore. Its streets are broad and straight, and generally cross each other at right angles. Niagara Square, from which eight streets radiate, is a handsome open quadrangle, surrounded by elegant private residences. The business portion of the city is near the lake and river. Wharves, elevators, and extensive warehouses line the harbor; the largest of the latter is that of the Central Railroad, used exclusively for its own consignments. At the back of these immense buildings flows the Erie Canal, with only narrow tow-paths between its waters and the lofty warehouses. The number of vessels continually arriving and

## ERIE RAILWAY ROUTE.

departing from this port is very great. Business is greatly facilitated by the elevators. There are thirty-one of these, which have an aggregate transfer capacity of 2,889,000 bushels per day, and a warehouse capacity of 7,415,000 bushels. Great numbers of cattle from the West are shipped from Buffalo both by water and by rail. The manufactures of Buffalo are of great extent and variety, employing several millions of capital and thousands of laborers. Among the principal public buildings is a large and handsome edifice at the corner of Seneca and Washington streets, in which is conducted the business of the Post-office, Custom House, and the United States Courts. It was constructed by the Federal Government at a cost of $140,000. The old and new court-houses, the former of which faces Lafayette Park on Main street, are fine buildings. The United States Arsenal is in Batavia street. There are also several admirably built markets in different parts of the city. In 1868, the city purchased the old water-works from the company who were the proprietors, and have since erected additional pumps on the Holly plan, which require no reservoir, and pump directly into the mains, and a high service supply is thus secured. The old reservoir has a capacity of 13,500,000 gallons. There are about seventy churches in Buffalo, many of which are spacious and handsome. The Roman Catholic Cathedral of St. Joseph is built entirely of stone, in an elegant and expensive style. It is without galleries, and at the back of the altar is a tripartite window of stained glass, manufactured at Munich, representing the birth, crucifixion, and ascension of the Saviour. The Protestant Episcopal Church of St. Paul is an imposing edifice, and has a chime of bells which cost $15,000. The principal cemetery is Forest Lawn, about three miles from the city. It is a spacious and well-chosen location, somewhat undulating in surface, and is tastefully laid out. The public schools have a high reputation. In the highest department a complete academic course is taught, excepting the classics. Number of children attending is about 21,000. The benevolent institutions are numerous and liberally sustained. Among the most prominent are the Buffalo Asylum for the Insane, intended to accommodate about 500 patients; the Providence Lunatic Asylum, in charge of the Sisters of Charity; the Buffalo General Hospital, the Charity Hospital, St. Francis Hospital, several Orphan Asylums and Homes for the Friendless and Aged, Deaf and Dumb

## ERIE RAILWAY ROUTE.

Asylum, Church Charity Foundation, Magdalen and Foundling Asylums, and numerous societies for mutual aid and benefit, and the promotion of special objects of amelioration and reform.

There are a number of libraries and literary and scientific associations, among which are the Historical Society, with a large and increasing library peculiarly rich in works on the early history of the city and Western New York; the Grosvenor Library; the Young Men's Association, with a library of over 20,000 volumes; the Buffalo Law Library, the German Young Men's Association and Library, the Young Men's Christian Association; the Buffalo Fine Arts Academy, with an elegant collection of paintings, sculpture, and other works of art; the Society of Natural History, with a valuable museum; the Mechanics' Institute, and the Medical Department of the University of Buffalo.

### NIAGARA FALLS BRANCH.

THIS branch of the Erie extends from Buffalo to Suspension Bridge, a distance of 25¼ miles, and connects the main line with Niagara Falls and the Great Western Railway of Canada, at Clifton, Canada. By means of it passengers by the Erie can reach Niagara Falls from New York without change of cars, in the splendid palace and sleeping cars, for which the railway is justly famous. Passengers for the east or west can also visit the falls and make through connections either way.

Since the construction of this branch, the Erie Railway has become the favorite line for tourists from New York and Philadelphia, making the round trip from these cities to Niagara Falls, The Thousand Islands, St. Lawrence River, Montreal, Quebec, White Mountains, Adirondacks, Lake Champlain, Lake George, Saratoga, etc. Philadelphia tourists either go *via* New York, or, leaving Philadelphia by the North Pennsylvania, pass without change of cars over the Lehigh Valley Railway, through Mauch Chunk ("the most picturesque of American towns," and an important center of the anthracite coal region), and connect with the Erie at Elmira.

During the season of summer travel, the Erie Railway Co. sells tickets for round trips at rates much less than the trips would cost by purchasing the tickets over each road separately. A great many

## ERIE RAILWAY ROUTE.

different combinations are issued, so that the traveler can select his route according to his inclination and convenience.

Thousands avail themselves of the convenience of this arrangement every season, and the route is annually increasing in popularity among tourists.

The actual point of intersection of the branch and the main lines is at East Buffalo, distant two miles from the Buffalo depot, but the local trains over the branch run from Buffalo to Clifton, and thus connect directly with the lines terminating at Buffalo and at Clifton on the Canada side of the Niagara.

### EAST BUFFALO.

*421 miles from New York. From Suspension Bridge,* 23¼.

This is the point of intersection of the main line and branch. It is within the limits of the city of Buffalo.

### MAIN STREET.

*426 miles from New York. From Suspension Bridge,* 18¼.

This station is at the crossing of Main street, Buffalo, and the R.R. It is within the limits of the city of Buffalo.

### TONAWANDA, Erie Co., N. Y.,

*432 miles from New York. From Suspension Bridge,* 12½.

This is an important village, situated on the banks of the Niagara River and both sides of the Tonawanda Creek at its mouth. It has a good harbor, and, being situated on the Erie Canal, quite a large amount of lumber and grain is here received and shipped eastward by the canal and railroads. It is the western terminus of the Canandaigua and Niagara Falls branch of the New York Central Railroad, which here connects with Buffalo and Niagara Falls branch of the same road.

Tonawanda is one of many places that narrowly escaped greatness. It was originally fixed upon for the western terminus of the Erie Canal. Buffalo finally secured the terminus, and with it, prosperity and greatness. Tonawanda, however, has a side cut for a river-lock, and an elevator, as well as a considerable lumber trade and some manufactures. The Indian name, Tonawanda (*Ta-nó-wan-deh*), is said to signify "At the Rapids."

# ERIE RAILWAY ROUTE.

Grand Island, opposite Tonawanda, was after the war of 1812 claimed by both the United States and Great Britain. The dispute as to which was the principal branch of the river was settled by a joint commission of the two governments in 1818.

The scheme of Major Mordecai M. Noah, to form a colony of Jews upon the island, is perhaps worthy of mention here, as an item of interest, although his attempt ended in failure. His idea was to purchase the island from the State, and found a city upon it, as refuge and resting-place for the people of his nation. For this purpose he memorialized the Legislature in 1820, setting forth the benefit the State would derive from the expected immigration.

But the Rabbis refused to encourage the scheme, and the Jews did r t seem to be anxious to settle, at least not here. Ararat was the name he proposed for the city he sought to found, but the monument set up by him has already tumbled down, and we doubt if the marble slab bearing its name and that of its founder, remains to be seen by the most curious of relic-seekers, if, indeed, the inhabitants retain either memory or tradition of its former existence.

### LA SALLE, Niagara Co., N. Y.

*438 miles from New York.   From Suspension Bridge,* 6¼.

A small post-office and station.

### NIAGARA FALLS, Niagara Co., N. Y.

*442 miles from New York.   From Suspension Bridge,* 2.

The world renowned cataract of Niagara gives name and interest to the place. Although but a village in population, its hotels are metropolitan in size and accommodations. The International is th largest, and situated close by the falls. Its table is excellent, and its rooms large and pleasant. Every year thousands of visitors flock to its banks to view, for once at least, a spectacle that ranks among the grandest which earth affords; while few travelers, whose route may chance to lead them near, will fail to snatch at least a few hours for the enjoyment of this sublime spectacle. The Niagara River, extending from Lake Erie to Lake Ontario, a distance of thirty miles, has a total fall of 334 feet; the greater part of the descent is confined to a distance of seven or eight miles, within which space are the grandest rapids and falls in the world. The rapids are so strong two miles

VIEW FROM PROSPECT POINT, NIAGARA FALLS.

above the falls as to entirely prevent navigation. There are three distinct cataracts. The Horse-shoe Falls, so called from its crescent shape, is by far the largest, and is in the direct course of the river; it is 2,000 feet wide and 154 feet high. The American Fall is 660 feet wide, and the Central Fall 243 feet, each having a fall of 163 feet. The two latter are separated from each other and from the former by Goat Island. The aggregate width of descending water is thus 2,900 feet, and the flow unceasing and nearly uniform in amount throughout the year. The amount of water discharged is computed to be 100,000,000 of tons per hour. More water passes in these fearful torrents in seven seconds than is conveyed through Croton aqueduct in twenty-four hours. At the Horse-shoe Fall the concussion of the falling waters with those in the depths below occasions a spray that veils the cataract two-thirds up its height. Above this impenetrable foam, to the height of fifty feet above the fall, a cloud of lighter spray rises, which, when the sun shines upon it in the proper direction, displays magnificent solar rainbows. Goat Island is midway between the American and Canada shores, in the midst of these boiling waters. It is separated from Bath by a narrow stream, and the latter island is connected with the American shore by an iron suspension bridge. It is said the first white person who ventured to cross the Rapids at Goat Island was Israel Putnam, in 1755. On the shore of the island, and beneath the smaller of the American falls, is the Cave of the Winds—a cavern formed by the decay of the softer substratum rock, whilst the hard superincumbent limestone still forms the roof. In front of the cave the center fall descends 240 feet in width, and compresses the air to such a degree that a fearful din continually reigns within this watery cavern, which is heightened by the foaming spray which rushes along the stony floor, mounts up the darkened sides, spreads over the roof, and thence descends in continued drenching showers. The most comprehensive view of the falls is obtained from the Canada side, where the three falls can be seen at the same time.

The Niagara River, below these stupendous falls, rushes through a deep chasm of 200 feet in height, spanned by two suspension bridges, one just below the falls, for passengers and carriages, from which they can be viewed most advantageously, and two miles below by the Great International Railway Suspension Bridge. Three miles below

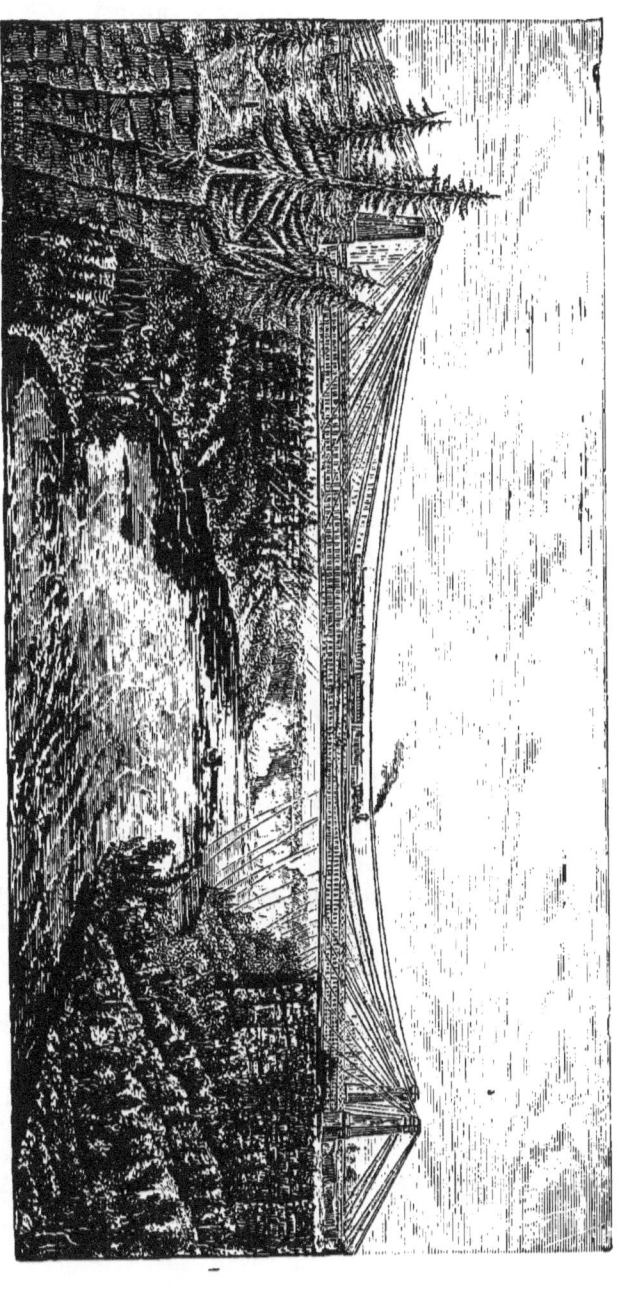

The Great International **RAILWAY SUSPENSION BRIDGE** Over the Niagara River
*In Full View of Niagara Falls,*
Connecting The Erie Railway and Great Western Railway of Canada.

the falls is the Whirlpool. It is caused by the abrupt turn of the river at this point, the waters of which rush with such violence against the cliff on the Canadian side as to occasion a severe reaction and rotary motion, drawing everything that flows down the river within the vortex. Below the Whirlpool is another series of rapids.

### SUSPENSION BRIDGE, Niagara Co., N. Y.,
*444½ miles from New York.*

An incorporated village, situated on Niagara River, two miles below the cataract, of which it commands a fine view. The International Suspension Bridge crosses the river at this point, and connects the Canadian railways with those of the States. The length of the bridge is 800 feet ; height above water, 230 feet ; width, 24 feet ; supported by four wire cables 9½ inches in diameter, and has a sustaining capacity of 12,400 tons. The towers are 88 feet on the American side, and 78 on the Canadian. Its total weight is 800 tons, and its cost $400,000. There are two floors, the upper for the railroad track and the lower for wagons. It was commenced in 1854, the late John A. Roebling, of Trenton, New Jersey, being the engineer. The east end of the bridge commands a fine view of the river above up to the Falls, and of the rapids under and below the bridge for three-quarters of a mile to the Whirlpool. The water of these rapids runs at the rate of twenty-five miles per hour, with breakers dashing from ten to twenty feet in height. When seen from the shore they present one of the grandest sights of the kind seen in the world, and the tourist has not seen all Niagara until he has stood on the shore 150 rods below the bridge. Deveaux College is a charitable institution under Episcopal management, and was established by the munificence of Hon. Samuel Deveaux, who bequeathed property amounting to upwards of $200,000 in value for that purpose.

### CLIFTON, Ontario, Canada,

The trains of the Erie Railway pass over Suspension Bridge in full view of Niagara Falls, and connect at Clifton with the Great Western Railway for Detroit and the West, and for Toronto *via* the Hamilton Division of the Great Western Railway.

ERIE RAILWAY ROUTE.

## ROCHESTER DIVISION OF THE ERIE RAILWAY.
### FROM CORNING TO ROCHESTER.

Trains over this route, after leaving Corning, take the line of the main road to Painted Post, then diverge to the north, passing up the valley of the Conhocton River through Steuben County, thence through Livingston County, between Conesus and Hemlock lakes, to Avon, from whence a branch extends to Batavia, connecting at that point with the Buffalo Branch of the Erie, and from Avon, through Monroe County to Rochester, connecting this important city directly with New York.

### CORNING,
291 *miles from New York. From Rochester*, 94. (See page 41.)

### PAINTED POST,
293 *miles from New York. From Rochester*, 93. (See page 41.)

### COOPER'S, Steuben Co., N. Y.,
296 *miles from New York. From Rochester*, 89.

A small post village near the northern line of the township, having a hotel, two churches, a flour-mill and an extensive rocking-chair manufactory. The mountain scenery in the vicinity is very fine. Wild game is abundant, principally deer. Stages run tri-weekly to Monterey, East Campbell, Townsend, Havana, and Watkins.

### CURTIS, Steuben Co., N. Y.,
299 *miles from New York. From Rochester*, 87.

A small place, containing two mills and a tannery.

### CAMPBELL, Steuben Co., N. Y.,
300 *miles from New York. From Rochester*, 85.

The surrounding country is broken and rough. Some of the hills rise from 300 to 500 feet above the valleys. It is near the junction of McNutt and Michigan creeks with Conhocton River.

### SAVONA, Steuben Co., N. Y.,
305 *miles from New York. From Rochester*, 80.

At the mouth of Mud Creek; contains two churches, a hotel, and 500 inhabitants. Stages run daily to Sonora, Bradford, and Tyrone, connecting at Tyrone with stage for Watkins.

ERIE RAILWAY ROUTE.

## BATH, Steuben Co., N. Y.,
### 311 *miles from New York. From Rochester,* 74.

This thriving village is situated on the left bank of the Conhocton Creek. It receives the trade of a rich agricultural district, and has a manufacturing and lumber business of considerable importance. Bath is one of the half shires of the county, Corning being the other. The court house at Bath is a commodious brick building, erected in 1828. An orphan asylum has been founded and built by Ira Davenport, at a cost of $200,000. The county poor-house is located upon a

SOLDIERS' HOME, BATH, N. Y.

farm of 214 acres, about two miles northeast of the village. Besides the county buildings, Bath contains about six churches, three banks, and several newspaper offices. There are also a number of mills and factories in the vicinity. It was incorporated in 1816, and has now a population of about 3,000. A narrow-gauge railroad, the Bath and Hammondsport Railroad, connects the Erie with the beautiful Keuka Lake at Hammondsport, in the heart of the grape-growing region of Central New York.

ERIE RAILWAY ROUTE.

**KANONA, Steuben Co., N. Y.,**
315 *miles from New York. From Rochester,* 71.

Formerly Kennedyville; is near the northern border of the township, at the mouth of Five Mile Creek, and contains two churches and forty houses.

**AVOCA, Steuben Co., N. Y.,**
319 *miles from New York. From Rochester,* 67.

Situated on the Conhocton, a little below the mouth of Ten Mile Creek; contains three churches, two public halls, two hotels, cheese-factories, an iron-foundry, and a flouring-mill. Population, 500.

**WALLACE'S, Steuben Co., N. Y.,**
322 *miles from New York. From Rochester,* 64.

Settled in 1800, is near the mouth of Twelve Mile Creek, and has two churches, saw-mill, grist-mill, etc.

**LIBERTY, Steuben Co., N. Y.,**
326 *miles from New York. From Rochester,* 59.

Situated in the center of the township, and on Conhocton River; contains two churches, and about 400 population. A considerable business is carried on here in hemlock lumber.

**BLOOD'S, Steuben Co., N. Y.,**
331 *miles from New York. From Rochester,* 55.

Near the northern border of the county; is an important station from its connection with the Canandaigua Lake route. A daily line of stages runs to Naples, at the head of the lake, and a steamer plies daily between the latter place and Canandaigua.

**WAYLAND, Steuben Co., N. Y.,**
337 *miles from New York. From Rochester,* 49.

This is in the north-western corner of the county. The land is rolling, and forms a portion of the watershed between Susquehanna River and Lake Ontario; the tributaries of the former reaching their final outlet in Chesapeake Bay, while those of the latter are discharged into the Gulf of St. Lawrence. Its highest summits are 1,600 to 1,800 feet above tide-water. The streams here are small creeks and brooks. Loon and Mud lakes are situated in a valley in the southern part of the town, and their waters flow in opposite directions. The outlet of the former is subterranean for half a mile,

ERIE RAILWAY ROUTE.

and when it again comes to the surface it is in sufficient volume to form a valuable mill-stream. The village contains fifty dwellings and two hotels. Stage connection with Dansville twice daily.

**SPRINGWATER**, Livingston Co., N. Y.,
341 *miles from New York. From Rochester*, 44.

North-west of the Center; contains two churches, a sash and blind factory, a saw-mill, two flour-mills, and about seventy houses.

**WEBSTER**, Livingston Co , N. Y.,
344 *miles from New York. From Rochester*, 41.

A pretty village, and the seat of the Webster Academy.

**CONESUS**, Livingston Co., N. Y.,
348 *miles from New York. From Rochester*, 37.

The township lies between Hemlock and Conesus lakes, two beautiful sheets of water. Marrowback Hills, in the eastern part, near Hemlock Lake, rise to about 1,200 feet above it. Conesus Center, near the station, has two churches, a saw and grist mill, and about forty houses. This is widely known as the "Round Pie Station," from the excellent small round pies kept for sale at the lunch-room of the station-house.

**SOUTH LIVONIA**, Livingston Co., N. Y.,
352 *miles from New York. From Rochester*, 34.

Four miles south from the Center; contains one church. Conesus and Hemlock lakes, near by, afford good fishing.

**LIVONIA**, Livingston Co., N. Y.,
356 *miles from New York. From Rochester*, 30.

The station has a manufactory of agricultural implements, and about 450 inhabitants. At this point we reach the eastern border of the rich Genesee Valley, and from this station more grain is shipped than from any other on the road. The Center, one and a half mile to the east, contains two churches and 250 inhabitants.

**HAMILTON'S**, Livingston Co., N. Y.,
358 *miles from New York. From Rochester*, 27.

This station, otherwise known as South Lima, is on the northern boundary of Livonia, at the corner of Avon and Lima. Small game abounds, and there is excellent pickerel fishing.

**AVON SPRINGS, Livingston Co., N. Y.,**
367 *miles from New York. From Rochester,* 18.

Avon is near the northern border of the county, and in the center of the richest agricultural district in the State. It is the most important station between Corning and Rochester. From this point the Erie Railway has two lines, one to Rochester, the other turning westward to Buffalo (see p. 70). The Dansville and Mount Morris Branch diverges here from the Erie (see p. 83), and runs southerly up the valley to Geneseo, Mount Morris, and Dansville, a distance of thirty miles. All trains stop at Avon for meals.

Avon is a watering-place of considerable note. Its strong sulphur springs are widely known. Long before the white man penetrated the forests of this valley these springs were well known to the Indians, who called them "Ganawagus," or "fetid waters." Nearly two hundred years ago De Nouville fought the first battle with the Indians of this territory, on the present site of Avon, and about a century later General Sullivan invaded this region, defeated the powerful Iroquois, and drove them from the valley.

Avon possesses a large park in the center of the village, which is the gift of the Wadsworth family, whose estate comprises thousands of acres of this fertile valley. The citizens of Avon have erected a "soldiers' monument" in the park which would do honor to a much more wealthy community.

There are many interesting drives in the vicinity of Avon. The "State Fisheries and Hatchery," under the management of Seth Green, are at Caledonia, only seven miles west, and are well worth visiting. A drive up the valley to Geneseo and Mount Morris introduces the traveler to the heart of the far-famed Genesee Valley. Geneseo was the home of General James Wadsworth, who fell at the Battle of the Wilderness, and is now the home of his son, the Hon. James Wadsworth.

**AVON SULPHUR SPRINGS.**

The sulphur waters of this locality have for years been recognized as among the most valued of their class in this country. Their medicinal qualities are similar to those of the celebrated Neudorf Spa of Germany. The following analysis of Avon spring waters, by Prof. J. B. Chilton, M.D., of New York, shows their properties:

In a gallon of 231 cubic inches:

| Solid contents. | Grains. | Gaseous contents. | Cubic Inch. |
|---|---|---|---|
| Carbonate of Lime | 29.33 | Sulphuretted Hydrogen | 10.02 |
| Chloride of Calcium | 8.41 | Nitrogen | 5.42 |
| Sulphate of Lime | 57.54 | Oxygen | .56 |
| Sulphate of Magnesia | 49.61 | Carbonic Acid | 3.92 |
| Sulphate of Soda | 13.73 | Traces of Iodide of Sodium. | |
| | 158.52 | | |

Traces of Iodine and Bromine.

The value of this water as a powerful remedial agent in a great variety of diseases is beyond dispute. Good authorities state that these waters are especially curative in *Liver Disorders, Abdominal Plethora, Malarial Affections of the Liver and Spleen, Chronic Malaria, Jaundice, Gall Stones, Incipient Tuberculosis, Rheumatism and Gout, Chronic Poisoning by Metals, Blood Poisons, Scrofula, Dartrous Affections of the Skin, Neuralgia, Hysteria, Chronic Bronchitis, Laryngitis, and Functional Derangements of the Uterine System.*

The nearest springs to the depot are those connected with the AVON SPRINGS HOTEL AND SANITARIUM, a popular resort at all seasons of the year, and admirably conducted by Dr. L. S. Hinkley & Co. Two distinct sulphur springs are within the twelve acres of beautiful grounds surrounding this Sanitarium.

A "NEW SANITARIUM" has recently been built upon the high ground in the eastern part of the village, near the park. Sulphur water is conveyed to this establishment in wooden pipes for drinking and bathing purposes. Dr. Cyrus Allen and Mr. J. D. Carson are the proprietors of this excellent institution, which is well patronized.

THE LIVINGSTON HOUSE is a first-class summer hotel, centrally located, and facing the public park. Dr. Nesbet, proprietor, has recently secured a well of sulphur water by boring to the depth of 133 feet.

"THE LOWER SPRINGS" are nearly a mile south-west of Avon village. Congress Hall is located here. Dr. Phelps, the proprietor, has done much to beautify the surroundings and make this a popular resort. Knickerbocker Hall is also located at "the Lower Springs."

### RUSH, Monroe Co., N. Y.
*371 miles from New York From Rochester, 14.*

This station, one mile west of West Rush, is the junction of the Genesee Valley, and Canandaigua, and Niagara Falls Railroads.

ERIE RAILWAY ROUTE.

**SCOTTSVILLE, Monroe Co., N. Y.,**
*373 miles from New York. From Rochester, 12.*

The village of Scottsville is one and a half miles west of the station, in the township of Wheatland, near where the Genesee Canal crosses the Genesee River. It has three churches, a Union school, extensive flouring-mills, plaster-mills, and a furnace. A stage runs between village and depot.

**HENRIETTA, Monroe Co., N. Y.,**
*377 miles from New York. From Rochester, 8.*

A small station. The village of West Henrietta is east of the station, and contains two large manufactories of wagons.

**RED CREEK, Monroe Co., N. Y.,**
*381 miles from New York. From Rochester, 4.*

**ROCHESTER, Monroe Co., N. Y.,**
*385 miles from New York.*

This is a modern city, having risen from the wilderness within about half a century. Its present population is about 90,000. The waters of the Genesee River, flowing to the northward from the Alleghany hills in the southern part of the State and Northern Pennsylvania, traverse the city and empty into Lake Ontario, eight miles distant. Within the city limits the river undergoes a descent of about 265 feet, falling into four distinct cataracts within the distance of two miles. The magnificent water-power thus afforded, located in the midst of one of the finest wheat-growing regions in the world, in connection with the facilities of transportation afforded by the Erie Canal, Lake Ontario, and the railways, have given a powerful impulse to the prosperity of the place, and it has become the most important flouring city in the world. Its product is from 600,000 to 1,000,000 barrels per annum. The Erie Canal crosses the Genesee by an aqueduct of cut stone, built at an expense of over $600,000. The Genesee Valley Canal, a tributary to the Erie, has its northern terminus here. Besides the Genesee Valley Railway, leased and operated by the Erie Railway Co., there are five sections of the New York Central Railway which converge at this point, viz., from Buffalo, from Niagara Falls, from Syracuse direct, from Syracuse by way of Canandaigua, and from Charlotte, at the mouth of Genesee

River. The Rochester and State Line R.R. runs southwest through Le Roy to the Pennsylvania line in Alleghany County. The Lake Shore Railroad crosses below the city. The city is regularly laid out with wide and handsome streets, of which many are lined with shade-trees. Main street on the east side, and Buffalo street on the

GENESEE FALLS, ROCHESTER, N. Y.

west side of the river, form by means of a stone bridge one continuous street, the "Broadway" of the city, lined with handsome stores, hotels, public buildings, etc. The suburbs are ornamented by numerous and elegant residences, surrounded by tasteful grounds and gardens. The different cataracts of the Genesee evidently formed at one time a single cascade, but the different degrees of hardness of the several rocks have caused an unequal retrograde movement

## ERIE RAILWAY ROUTE.

of the falls, until they have assumed their present position. At the Upper Falls, just north of the New York Central Railway bridge, the water descends 96 feet over the perpendicular face of Niagara limestone, underlaid by shale. At this place the noted Sam Patch made his last and fatal leap. Below the Upper Falls the river flows between nearly perpendicular walls about one and three-quarter miles to the Middle Falls, where it has a descent of 25 feet. One hundred rods below it descends 84 feet at the Lower Falls, over a ledge of Medina sandstone to the level of Lake Ontario. The water-power thus produced is immense, and good use is made of it in the various and important manufactories carried on here. Besides the large flouring-mills, some twenty-four in number, there are extensive manufactories of flour barrels, of axes and edge-tools, of coaches and carriages, of boots and shoes, of chairs, cotton factories, machine-shops, a large safe and scale manufactory, furnaces, breweries, boat-yards, carpet factories, paper-mills, saw-mills, planing-mills, tanneries, rifle-manufactories, soap and candle factories, etc. The city takes rank among the first manufacturing towns of the State. The trade and commerce of the city is very important, as will be perceived when we consider the immense quantity of flour exported, and the extensive manufacturing carried on. The local trade is far from insignificant, as nearly half a million population are within two hours' travel of the city. The greatest nurseries of America are here. Thousands of acres, within five miles of the city, are devoted to the culture of fruit-trees, and millions of trees are annually sent abroad to other States and foreign lands. The annual product of these nurseries is $2,000,000. There are many miles of improved streets, and of excellent sewerage. Horse-railroads connect the different portions of the city. There are twelve spacious parks, and four elegant bridges over the Genesee. The court-house and city hall cost $80,000. The University of the City of Rochester, is located on a tract of twelve acres just east of the city limits, near the Central Railway. It has a valuable library, and fine mineralogical cabinet. Connected with it is the Baptist Theological Seminary. This has a German department, and includes in its library 4,600 volumes, formerly the property of Dr. Aug. Neander, the German religious historian. The Western House of Refuge, a State reform-school for vicious boys, is a large and imposing edifice near the

## ERIE RAILWAY ROUTE.

Rochester and Niagara Falls Railway. There are usually about 400 inmates, who are required to labor during certain hours of the day, and to devote a certain amount of time to study. There are two large hospitals, St. Mary's, under the management of the Sisters of Charity, the other a city institution. Mount Hope Cemetery is located in Brighton, near the south line of the city, on Mount Hope, a beautiful eminence overlooking the city. It is laid out in excellent taste, and is one of the finest rural cemeteries in the country. Visitors to Rochester should not fail to visit it. A very inadequate idea of the city is gained by passing through in the cars: Drives on its fine avenues and strolls in its parks will well repay the tourist.

### AVON TO BUFFALO.

This route, with that from Corning to Avon, comprises the Buffalo, New York, and Erie Railway, leased and operated by the Erie Railway Co.

**CALEDONIA, Livingston Co., N. Y.**

*374 miles from New York. From Buffalo, 59.*

A village of 700 inhabitants. There are two good hotels. The manufacturing enterprises of the town are extensive and numerous, and a large shipping business is done, the station being a depot for several interior villages. The State Hatching Ponds, for the artificial propagation of fish, are situated here, and are under the charge of Seth Green, well known for the intelligent interest he has taken in this subject. Stage to Mumford, Monroe County, twice daily.

**LEROY, Genesee Co., N. Y.**

*381 miles from New York. From Buffalo, 52.*

This pleasant and thriving village is finely located on Oatka Creek, in the center of the township, and is one of the most beautiful in Western New York. Gypsum and Onondaga limestone, for building purposes, are obtained in this town. In the eastern part, south of the creek, is an extensive tract of oak openings, covered thickly with stone, and hard to cultivate. The village contains a bank, a newspaper office, and a female seminary. Ingham University is a school of great reputation, and Leroy Academy a flourishing institution. The stone building near the railroad, east of the station, was built for a car-shop, but is now a malt-house.

# ERIE RAILWAY ROUTE.

### STAFFORD, Genesee Co., N. Y.,
### 386 *miles from New York.  From Buffalo*, 47.

The village lies on Black Creek, near the center of the township, contains three churches, and a population of 450. The station lies equidistant between the villages of Stafford and Morganville.

### BATAVIA, Genesee Co., N. Y.,
### 396 *miles from New York.  From Buffalo*, 37.

Was settled in the early part of the century. Five branches of the Central Railroad converge here—from Albany by Rochester, from Albany by Canandaigua, from Buffalo, from Niagara Falls and Canada, and from Attica. The village contains five churches, a State arsenal, a Union school, and several newspapers are published, the first started in 1807. It has a number of manufacturing establishments, and a population of 3,000. It was here that the first meeting to advocate the construction of the Erie Canal was held in 1809. The war of 1812 put an end to the agitation of the subject, but it was renewed after peace was proclaimed. The abduction of Morgan, the alleged betrayer of the secrets of Freemasonry took place here. He came to Batavia to write and print his work. He made no secret of his work, and soon an excitement was raised, during which, on the pretence of taking him to Canandaigua for trial for money loaned him, he was carried off, none knew where. Some say he was executed at the mouth of Niagara River. The publication went on under one Miller. A civil war arose ; men armed with clubs met to demolish the office, but a cannon in the hands of the citizens kept them off until the book was published, when violence ceased. The "Oak Orchard Acid Springs" are situated about twelve miles northwest of the station, in the town of Alabama, on Oak Orchard Creek. These curious springs are nine in number, all located within a circle fifty rods in diameter ; three of them issuing from a mound within ten feet from each other. In no two of them is the water alike. They are found, by analysis, to contain, besides other mineral substances, a quantity of free sulphuric acid. Large quantities of the water are bottled and sold for medicinal purposes. Batavia was the residence of Dean Richmond, who was the president of the New York Central R. R. Co. at the time of his death.

ERIE RAILWAY ROUTE.

**ALEXANDER, Genesee Co., N. Y.,**
404 *miles from New York. From Buffalo,* 29.

Contains a flouring-mill, three churches, and the Genesee and Wyoming Seminary, founded in 1834 by Samuel Benedict and Henry Hawkins. Its main building is built of stone, and will accommodate 300 students.

For a description of Attica and the stations beyond to Buffalo, see Buffalo Division, page 49.

## MINOR BRANCHES OF THE ERIE RAILWAY.

### PATERSON AND NEWARK BRANCH.

This branch of the Erie Railway extends from New York to Paterson *via* Newark (20 miles). It leaves the main line just after passing through the Bergen Tunnel, and crosses the Hackensack River, the meadows west, and the Passaic River at the northern limit of Newark.

**NEWARK, Essex Co., N. J.,**
9 *miles from New York. From Paterson,* 11.

On the Passaic River. This is the most important city in the State of New Jersey, and thirteenth in rank in the Union. It was founded in 1666 by Puritans, who laid out much of what is now the old portion of the city. Newark is the capital of Essex County, and is especially noted for the variety and extent of its manufacturing establishments, which are numbered by hundreds. The banking and other moneyed institutions are on a commensurate scale, and the buildings devoted to these interests are as handsome as any in the country. During the Revolutionary War, the contending armies frequently occupied Newark. After the establishment of peace the town grew slowly, until the completion of the Morris Canal and the railways, when it rapidly increased in population and importance.

Its railroad communication with New York affords every facility for travel and traffic to and from the great metropolis. Besides the Erie Railway, three other railroads connect the city with New York, viz., the Pennsylvania Central, the Newark and New York and the Newark and Elizabeth branches of the Central Railroad of New Jersey

ERIE RAILWAY ROUTE.

and the Delaware, Lackawanna and Western, running in all nearly 200 trains daily. Newark has a number of fine parks and streets. Its main avenue, Broad street, is 132 feet wide. Aaron Burr was a native of Newark. The late Gen. Phil. Kearney resided here on the bank of the Passaic. On the opposite shore from the "Kearney Place" stands the ancient house immortalized by Washington Irving in the *Salmagundi*, under the title of "Cockloft Hall."

### WOODSIDE, Essex Co., N. J.,
*10 miles from New York. From Paterson, 10.*

A pleasant suburban village.

### BELLVILLE, Essex Co., N., J.,
*11 miles from New York From Paterson, 9.*

This place, lying on the northern border of the city of Newark, is a rapidly growing suburban city, drawing its increasing population from the overflowing populations of Newark and New York.

Bellville is the location of the water works which supply Jersey City with hydrant water. The remaining stations of Essex, Avondale, Stitts, Franklin, Peru, and Centerville are mainly populated by persons doing business in New York, who go and return daily. They are all pleasant places, with attractive scenery along the banks of the Passaic River. At Paterson the main line is again joined.

## NORTHERN RAILROAD OF NEW JERSEY.
*New York to Nyack, 29 miles.*

This branch of the Erie Railway diverges from the main line immediately west of the Bergen Tunnel, and runs in a northerly direction to Nyack, on the Hudson, in Rockland County, New York, the railroad traversing the Hackensack meadows until it reaches New Durham, where it enters the upland region. The various villages along this route are largely inhabited by the families of people who do business in New York City, and ride to and fro every day. The trains are run at hours to accommodate this class of travel, which furnishes a very large percentage of the passenger traffic, and is rapidly increasing. New Durham, Granton, Ridgefield, and Leonia, are small stations, and the first one of importance is

ERIE RAILWAY ROUTE.

### ENGLEWOOD, Bergen Co., N. J.,
*14 miles from New York. From Nyack, 15.*

This is one of the handsomest villages in the State, and contains a large number of splendid private residences, several summer hotels, elegant church buildings, etc. It is a favorite summer residence for New Yorkers. The villages of Highland, Tenafly, Cresskill, Closter, and Norwood, are all attractive and beautiful places, growing fast in population and wealth, and situated in healthy and picturesque locations. Churches and schools are numerous, many of the buildings being fine specimens of architecture.

### TAPPAN, Rockland Co., N. Y.,
*23 miles from New York. From Nyack, 6.*

The village is called Tappantown, and is a small but pleasant place. It was the scene of the trial and execution of Major André in 1780. In 1831 his remains were removed to England, under the direction of the British Consul at New York.

Passing Sparkill, where connection is made for Piermont, the terminus of the road is reached at

### NYACK, Rockland Co., N. Y.,
*29 miles from New York.*

This is the largest village in the county, and although not a place of much business, is rapidly growing. Its romantic situation, and readiness of access from New York City, both by steamers on the Hudson River, and the railroad, are the causes of its prosperity. A large number of persons make this their home, going to the great city every morning and returning at night. In the summer season it is a favorite resort, and the several large hotels in the vicinity are crowded with boarders. There is a new and handsome school building in the village, and several churches. The roads in the vicinity are excellent, and afford opportunities for most romantic drives.

ERIE RAILWAY ROUTE.

## NEWBURGH (SHORT-CUT) BRANCH.
*From Turner's to Newburgh, 18 miles.*

This branch skirts the western base of the Highlands of the Hudson. The first station is

### CENTRAL VALLEY, Orange Co., N. Y.,
*48 miles from New York.*

This place is directly among the Highlands, and distant about ten miles from West Point. There is a good hotel, and quite a number of private boarding-houses. There are also several churches.

### HIGHLAND MILLS, Orange Co., N. Y.,
*50 miles from New York.*

A station in a neighborhood which is a favorite summer resort. Cromwell Lake, one mile distant, having one of the largest summer hotels in the country. The stations of Valley and Mountainville are in the vicinity of the Cornwall Mineral Springs, whose waters are celebrated for their curative qualities.

### CORNWALL, Orange Co., N. Y.,
*56 miles from New York.*

The numerous and picturesque lakelets, streams, and mountains, and the grand and romantic scenery around this favored place, have made it a favorite resort for thousands during the summer months. The village proper is about three miles from the depot, and is reached by stages connecting with every train. Here was the home of the late N. P. Willis, whose life was prolonged many years by his residence in the healthful region, he having been a confirmed consumptive when he sought the place. Cornwall is now regularly recommended to sufferers from pulmonary complaints by physicians.

### NEW WINDSOR, Orange Co., N. Y.,
*61 miles from New York.*

The scenery and drives in this neighborhood are fully equal to any other in the Highland region. Idlewild, the home of the late N. P. Willis, is distant two and a half miles, and within a radius of three miles from the station are many hotels and summer boarding-houses. Between this point and Newburgh the scenery is grand and imposing. The railway descends through a gorge in the mountain by a long grade to the level of the Hudson.

HUDSON RIVER AT WEST POINT, LOOKING SOUTH.
CRANSTON'S HOTEL IN THE DISTANCE.

ERIE RAILWAY ROUTE.

## NEWBURGH, Orange Co., N. Y.,
### 63 *miles from New York.*

Newburgh is a prosperous city of 20,000 inhabitants, and is one of the first settlements of the State, having been founded in 1709. It lies upon the sloping bank of the river, and rises about 130 feet to a plateau, now the finest part of the city. Beyond this there is another rise to a level of 190 feet, and still further west a greater rise until it reaches an elevation of about 300 feet. It is connected with Fishkill station on the Hudson River Railroad by a steam ferry, and the steamboats on the Hudson River make a landing here. The city is associated with revolutionary history, from having been the headquarters of the patriot army during the closing years of the war. The house occupied by Washington stands in the south part of the city, and is now the property of the State, and is open to visitors. The city is supplied with an abundance of water, has many retail stores, excellent schools, churches of all denominations, a theological seminary belonging to the United Presbyterians, and a considerable amount of manufactures, trade, and commerce.

## THE WARWICK BRANCH.
### *From Greycourt to Warwick,* 10 *miles.*

This branch extends south ten miles from Greycourt through East Chester, Sugar Loaf Lake, and Stone Bridge, which are small stations. This section of Orange County dates its settlement among the earliest in the interior of the State. In 1712 settlement was begun by the proprietors of the Wawayanda Patent, and the name of Warwick given to the tract. The first mill was erected in 1760. A great variety of minerals are found in this neighborhood, and iron furnaces are operated by the Sterling Iron Company. The country has all the characteristics belonging to a wild and mountainous region. There are a number of beautiful lakes abounding with fish. The terminus of the branch is at Warwick, Orange Co., N. Y., a prosperous village of a thousand inhabitants. It is situated on Wawayanda Creek, and has a newspaper, a bank, an academy, and several churches.

ERIE RAILWAY ROUTE.

## Pine Island Branch.
*From Goshen to Pine Island,* 12 *miles.*

This branch runs in a southerly direction from Goshen to Pine Island, a short distance north of the New Jersey State line. The railroad is projected beyond this point to Deckertown, New Jersey, and is intended, when finished, to connect with lines of railroad running to the coal regions of Eastern Pennsylvania. The first station is Orange Farm, and the next is

### FLORIDA, Orange Co., N. Y.,
*65 miles from New York.*

Located in the center of a rich agricultural district, and is a very handsome village. The Seward Institute, founded here by the father of the late Hon. Wm. H. Seward, is in a prosperous condition. In Mount Eve, some three miles southwest of Florida, is a natural cave of considerable size; fourteen rooms have been explored and found to contain many curiosities. There are good hotels in this village, and excellent fishing and gunning in the neighborhood.

### BIG ISLAND and PINE ISLAND, Orange Co., N. Y.

In this portion of the county are extensive levels called the Drowned Lands. Several eminences in the midst of these meadows are denominated islands, which will explain the singular titles of these inland villages.

At New Paltz Station, on the Wallkill Valley Railroad (87 miles from New York), there is stage connection with Lake Mohonk (9 miles), and Lake Minnewaska (16 miles). These lakes are in the summits of the highest peak of the Shawangunk Mountains, and are noted summer resorts. A large hotel at each one annually accommodates hundreds of guests.

ERIE RAILWAY ROUTE.

## MONTGOMERY BRANCH.

*From Goshen to Montgomery, 10 miles.*
This branch follows the valley of the Wallkill River through scenery of great natural beauty.

### MONTGOMERY, Orange Co., N. Y.,
### 69 *miles from New York.*

Is the first stopping-place. This is a famous resort for sportsmen, and a noted place for blooded stock. The population is about 1,000. There is an academy and a newspaper office, and two churches. From Montgomery the Wallkill Valley Railroad extends in direct connection with the Erie, to Kempton, N. Y., whence easy communication is had with the best Catskill region, *via* Ulster and Delaware Railroad to Stamford, Delaware County. This Erie route to the Catskills is the only all-rail route between New York and the favorite summer resorts of these mountains.

## PORT JERVIS AND MONTICELLO RAILROAD.

*From Port Jervis to Monticello, 24 miles.*
This road is twenty-four miles in length, and runs from Port Jervis through Huguenot, Rose Point, and Paradise, in Orange County, and Oakland, Hartwood, Gilmans, and Barnums, in Sullivan County. These are all unimportant places in themselves, the settlements being small; but a large amount of dairy and other products are shipped from them to market. Mongaup Falls, six miles from Hartwood, are worthy of note. The river here falls into a chasm seventy feet deep, and the banks below the falls are more than 100 feet high.

### MONTICELLO, Sullivan Co., N. Y.,

The county seat of Sullivan County. Population about 1,200. It is situated upon a ridge of highlands 1,387 feet above tide-water. The court-house, jail, clerk's and surrogates offices are located here; there are several churches, a bank, and good hotels. Nine miles from Monticello is White Lake, a pleasant resort, with accommodations for a large number of visitors. Stages connect with all trains.

ERIE RAILWAY ROUTE.

## The Honesdale Branch.

*From Lackawaxen to Honesdale, 25 miles.*

This branch leaves the main line at Lackawaxen. The scenery in the vicinity is very picturesque and beautiful. The Lackawaxen River, which takes its rise in the Moosic Mountains, here joins the Delaware. Down this stream the first anthracite coal ever mined in the Lackawanna region was floated to market. The rude ark which bore the adventurous Maurice Wurts, was the pioneer of the innumerable fleet of boats that have since found their way, laden with the treasure of the mountains, through the Delaware and Hudson Canal.

Rowlands, Millville and Kimble's are small stations, principally resorted to by sportsmen, the Honesdale Branch extending through the fine game and fishing region of northern Pike County. Millville, 118 miles from New York, is important as being the station for Blooming Grove Park, seven miles distant, in the Pike County wilderness. The Park comprises 12,000 acres of forest, lake and stream, and belongs to an association of New York sportsmen. They have a fine club house on the shores of Lake Giles, one of eight mountain lakes on their property. Several hundred acres have been enclosed as a game preserve, and great care is taken to protect the deer and other game animals during the season when they are rearing their young. The lakes and streams have been stocked with trout, black bass, and other fish, and the association has thus secured within easy access of New York, a hunter's and fisherman's paradise.

**HAWLEY, Wayne Co., Pa.**
*126 miles from New York.*

An important manufacturing place, among its interests being silk and glass and lumber manufactories. The place is connected with the anthracite coal fields by the Pennsylvania Coal Company's Gravity Railroad. This road is one of the finest excursion routes in America. It extends to Scranton, over a mountain range 2,000 feet high, a distance of 35 miles. The Wallen Paupack Falls are a series of magnificent cataracts near the village. The Erie is building a branch from Hawley to Pittston in the anthracite coal fields.

**WHITE MILLS, Wayne Co., Pa.**
*130 miles from New York.*

A picturesque village, where are located the celebrated Dorflinger Cut Glass Works.

ERIE RAILWAY ROUTE.

**HONESDALE, Wayne Co., Penn.,**

*From New York, 135 miles.   From Lackawaxen, 25.*

This is the county-seat, and contains the court-house and jail There are a number of churches, some of which are quite handsome. There is no coal mined in the immediate vicinity of Honesdale, but it is the largest coal-storing depot in the world. It has also the distinction of being the place where, in 1829, the first locomotive engine was run in America. The population is about 5,000. There are many handsome private residences. The streets are beautifully shaded with rows of maples, which give a very attractive appearance to the place. At Honesdale connection is made with the Delaware and Hudson Canal Company's Gravity Railroad for Carbondale and Scranton. Like the Gravity road from Hawley, this road offers one of the most novel and pleasurable trips to be enjoyed in this country. The Moosic Mountains form one of the loftiest spurs of the Alleghenies. Some of the peaks are 2,500 feet in height. The range is wild and rugged, and nowhere else in the State of Pennsylvania is the scenery grander or more diversified. Scaling its summits, spanning its chasms, and threading its dense forests, are these two novel railroads. These roads are operated by an ingenious system of inclined planes, up and down the mountain, there being no locomotive smoke nor cinders to annoy the tourists. The delightful character of a ride over these gravity roads cannot be conveyed by words. There is nothing like it in this country. The highest point on this road is 2,000 feet, and from the car windows the Catskill Mountains may be seen, sixty miles away. Lakes, waterfalls, glens, and valleys make these two excursions by gravity unrivaled. The Erie Railway Company has made every arrrangement to introduce these roads to the public.

## THE BRADFORD BRANCH.

Ten years ago the twenty-four miles of road extending from Carrolton, on the Western Division, to the then unknown hamlet of Gilesville (now Buttsville), Pa., was returning a fair revenue to the Erie Company mainly from the lumber trade. Petroleum was discovered at Bradford in 1875, and a year or so later a great rush set in to that place from all parts of the country. The receipts of the

## ERIE RAILWAY ROUTE.

railroad became larger in one day than they had ever been in a month. Bradford and its surroundings became the greatest oil-producing region the world had ever known. In 1880 the population of Bradford, which in 1875 was an insignificant lumbering village of two or three hundred inhabitants, had increased to 10,000. It had become the center of an oil region producing between 70,000 and 75,000 barrels of petroleum a day. It is now one of the finest cities in the State, and its prosperity is assured independently of the oil business, which is nevertheless the present great source of its importance. Millions of barrels of oil change hands daily on the Bradford Exchange, and the "princes" of the business have their headquarters in the city. This region is one presenting endless attractions to the tourist and sight-seer. The oil wells, spouting their thousands of barrels of "the world's light;" the network of pipe-lines by which the oil is distributed throughout the region; the immense iron receptacles for the oil, in which are at present stored over 30,000,000 barrels, for which there is no demand; the numerous narrow-gauge railroads that radiate in all directions through the picturesque region; and the wonderful natural gas, brought from the depths of the earth, and affording not only light but heat for the city and surrounding towns, are novelties and marvels which can be seen to such an extent nowhere else in the world. The buildings, both public and private, in Bradford, are of a superior class, and give evidence that they were not erected in expectation that their usefulness would depend on the existence of oil in the district.

Besides Bradford, the oil business called into importance the stations of Limestone, Babcock, Kendale, Delgolios, Lewis Run, Big Shanty, Crawford's, Alton, and Buttsville (formerly Gilesville).

There are about 11,000 oil wells in the Bradford field, producing now nearly 40,000 barrels of oil a day, the oil deposit growing less and less.

The Erie Railway has extended the Bradford Branch from Buttsville to Johnsonburg, on the Philadelphia and Erie Division of the Pennsylvania Railroad. This work necessitated the construction of an iron bridge over a ravine near Alton, which is over 300 feet high, and 2,500 feet long. This is the highest railroad bridge in the world. Important connections are obtained at Johnsonburg with the great bituminous coal fields of Pennsylvania, the lower oil regions, and the iron districts of Western Pennsylvania.

ERIE RAILWAY ROUTE.

## THE NEW YORK, PENNSYLVANIA AND OHIO RAILROAD.
### SALAMANCA, N. Y., TO DAYTON, O.

This road, which is now really a continuation of the Erie Railway, connects with the latter at Salamanca. Trains run through both ways without change of cars. The route of the N. Y., P. & O. extends from its initial point at Salamanca in a south-westerly direction, through New York, Western Pennsylvania, and Ohio, to Dayton, Ohio, a distance of 389 miles, whence the through trains are run over the line of the Cincinnati, Dayton, & Hamilton Railroad, fifty-nine miles to Cincinnati. After leaving Salamanca, which derives its chief importance from being the point of junction with the Erie, the next station of note is Jamestown, Chautauqua County, New York, situated near the beautiful Chautauqua Lake. At Corry, sixty-one miles west from Salamanca, the route of the road is through the celebrated oil-regions of Pennsylvania; connection is here made for Titusville, Pa. At Meadville, Pa, the Franklin branch diverges for Reno and Oil City, distant thirty-six miles. At Transfer, a small station, connection is made with the Erie & Pittsburg Railroad. At Shenango, with the Shenango & Allegheny Railroad, for Greenville. At Leavittsburg the Mahoning Division diverges for Cleveland, Youngstown, and Sharon, Pa. At Ravenna connection is made with the Cleveland & Pittsburg Railroad. At Akron, with the Cleveland, Mount Vernon, & Delaware Railroad, for Orrville, Millersburg, etc. At Russell, with the Cleveland, Tusc. Valley & Wh. Railroad. At Mansfield, a flourishing town in Richland County, Ohio, the Pittsburg, Fort Wayne, & Chicago, and the Baltimore & Ohio Railroad connect. At Galion connection is made with the Cleveland, Columbus, Cincinnati, & Indianapolis Railway. At Urbana with the Pittsburgh, Cincinnati, & St. Louis Railway, for Indianapolis, and at Dayton with the Cincinnati, Hamilton, & Dayton Railroad, for Cincinnati. The Erie is now running a "Limited Express" through from New York to Cincinnati and St. Louis, with fast time, leaving New York at 6 P. M. daily and arriving in Cincinnati at 8.20 P. M. next day, and in St. Louis at 8.40 A. M. second day.

ERIE RAILWAY ROUTE.

## CHICAGO AND ATLANTIC RAILWAY.

### MARIAN, OHIO, TO CHICAGO.

This is a most substantially constructed and elegantly equipped railway, just completed in the interest of the Erie. It joins the New York, Pennsylvania and Ohio at Marian, and the entire 269 miles between that point and Chicago is almost devoid of grade, and is 97 per cent. of straight line—a literal "bee line." The Chicago and Atlantic is the last link in the chain that gives the Erie a through line between New York and Chicago, and solid Pullman trains are run the entire distance. Connections are made at Lima with the Cincinnati, Hamilton and Dayton; at Decatur with the Grand Rapids and Indiana Railroad; at Kingsland with the Fort Wayne, Cincinnati and Louisville Railway, and the Lake Shore and Michigan Southern Railway; at Union and Newton with the Wabash, St. Louis and Pacific Railroad; and at Rochester with the Jeffersonville, Madison and Indianapolis Railway.

## Dansville and Mt. Morris Branch.

This branch runs from Avon to Dansville, 30 miles, through the famous Genesee Valley to Mt. Morris, whence it follows the Canaseraga, a tributary of the Genesee River. The first station after leaving Avon is South Avon, an agricultural village in the southern part of Avon township.

**GENESEO, Livingston Co., N. Y.,**
Formerly called Big Tree, from an immense oak tree that stood on the banks of the river; was incorporated in 1832. It is the county-seat. The court-house is beautifully located in the north part of the village. The village contains an insane asylum, the Geneseo Normal and Training School, Geneseo Academy, Wadsworth Library, founded by James Wadsworth, several churches, the county court-house, jail, and clerk's office, and several industrial enter-

STATE NORMAL SCHOOL, GENESEO, N. Y.

prises. Population about 2,500. The Wadsworth homesteads, in the north and south portions of the village, are surrounded with beautiful groves and lawns, and are attractive villas.

After leaving Geneseo the next station is Cuylerville, an incorporated village of about 400 inhabitants, one mile west of the station.

ERIE RAILWAY ROUTE.

### MT. MORRIS, Livingston Co., N. Y.
*382 miles from New York.   From Dansville, 15.   Pop., 2,500*

Named from Robert Morris, the great financier of the Revolutionary War, was incorporated in 1835. It is situated on the Genesee Valley Canal, which at this point is over 1,100 feet above tidewater, and about 600 feet above the Erie Canal at Rochester. Mt. Morris is a thriving village, containing several churches, a female high-school, banks, mills, etc. Passing *Sonyea* and *McNair*, unimportant stations, we arrive at

### DANSVILLE, Livingston Co., N. Y.
*397 miles from New York*

The terminus of the railroad, and a flourishing incorporated village of about 5,000 inhabitants, situated in the well-known Genesee Valley, celebrated for its fertility and salubrious climate. It contains several churches, excellent schools, large stores, several banks; paper, flour, plaster mills; sash factories, breweries and other industries. The Dansville Seminary, under the direction of the Methodist Episcopal Church, is a flourishing institution, and the leading school of hygiene in the country. Numerous glens, cascades, lakelets, and brooks surround the village, making Dansville a very popular summer resort for those who would rest and free themselves from the excitement of the fashionable watering-places.

THE DANSVILLE SANATORIUM, Our Home on the Hillside, is situated delightfully upon the eastern hill about half a mile above the village and 150 feet above its main street. The institution comprises a large new fire-proof central building with piazzas, a handsome chapel, and a number of attractive cottages scattered about the ground; trees, shrubs, flowers; walks, artistically arranged, add to the beauty of the place and the comfort of the guests, and the massive mountain rising abruptly to the height of a thousand feet behind the Home adds grandeur to the beauty of the place. This section of country abounds in the most delightful drives. The water supply is of the purest and most abundant character. The air is bracing, perfectly free from malaria; the drainage and hygienic surroundings of the place are excellent. The methods employed embrace the rational use of all the best known agencies for the restoration of the sick to health. The excellence of the accommoda-

# DANSVILLE SANATORIUM.

## OUR HOME ON THE HILLSIDE,
### DANSVILLE, LIVINGSTON CO., N. Y.

The Sanatorium, widely known as "Our Home on the Hillside," an unrivaled resort for invalids or persons seeking rest and quiet. The largest establishment of the kind in the world. New main building *absolutely fire-proof*, with every sanitary convenience. In charge of medical faculty composed of graduates from regular medical colleges, several of whom have had extended European opportunities for study and practice. Massage, Swedish movements, inunction, electricity, light gymnastics, and all the most approved forms of baths, including Moller Thermo-Electric, Turkish, Russian and Roman, employed according to indications in individual cases. Situation unsurpassed for health and rural beauty. No Malaria—absolutely purity of air and water. Large woodland park and magnificent scenery. On direct line of D. L. & W. R. R., and branch of Erie. Open all the year. For Circulars address,

*The Sanatorium, Dansville, Livingston Co., N. Y.*

tions now offered to the public by the new Sanatorium will be highly appreciated by people who have long sought an institution of this kind with such complete arrangements and unexcelled advantages. This is now the largest and the only absolutely fire-proof building of the kind in the world. The Sanatorium is in charge of a competent corps of regularly educated physicians, and affords excellent advantages for invalids and over-taxed professional and business men who wish to rest and recuperate during the vacation months of the year.

## Every Owner of Harness

SHOULD GIVE

## FRANK MILLER'S
# HARNESS DRESSING
### A TRIAL.

It is Just What You Want!

Gives a beautiful finish, and is not in the least injurious to Leather.

Ask your Harness Maker for it and be sure to get the Genuine.

# FRANK MILLER & SONS,
### ESTABLISHED IN 1838.
## NEW YORK AND LONDON.

ERIE RAILWAY ROUTE.

## THE ROUTE OF THE ST. LAWRENCE RIVER.

After the tourist has completed his visit at Niagara, he should continue his route down the St. Lawrence River, to Montreal and Quebec. This majestic river affords one of the most charming tours to be found on the Western Continent; and he is far from being an American tourist who has not sailed across Lake Ontario into the St. Lawrence, through the beautiful Thousand Islands and down the wild and boisterous Rapids to the metropolis of Canada, and the quaint historic city of Quebec. No tour of the same distance in the world presents a combination of such grand, picturesque, and historic interest—together with so many of the comforts of traveling, as the tour of the St. Lawrence. Secure your passage tickets *via* the Richelieu and Ontario Navigation Co.'s steamers, at the Company's office, 4 International Block, Niagara Falls, *via* Hamilton and Toronto to Quebec, for these are the finest steamers on the Lake, make the trip in the shortest time, and afford their passengers the best accommodations. Travelers with tickets by this line have the choice of pursuing the whole journey by steamer, or making a part of the trip *via* the Grand Trunk Railway. Hamilton, at the head of Burlington Bay, is the starting point of the R. & O. N. Co.'s "Royal Mail Line" steamers which leave daily, and is the only point where first choice of staterooms can be made. Take the Great Western Railway from Niagara Falls, and stop at the Royal Hotel, Hamilton, or the Ocean House, Burlington Beach, the Long Branch of Canada; or take the cars to Lewiston, N. Y., and thence the steamer down the rapid Niagara River, ten miles to Niagara Town, Canada; thence past Forts Niagara, on the United States, and Massasauga on the Canadian shore, across Lake Ontario, forty miles, to Toronto. At Toronto take the steamer of the R. & O. N. Co., or the Grand Trunk Railway, as he may choose, to Kingston, touching at Port Hope, Coburg, and Belleville, and from Kingston the route is by steamer alone. Near Kingston begin the Thousand Islands, which extend nearly fifty miles east of Brockville. Over 1,800 islands of variable shapes, covered with trees and rocks, are scattered through this reach of fifty miles of river, and as the steamer glides through the narrow channels, the scene changes into a thousand different aspects with kaleidoscopic rapidity and variety. Continuing our journey, we touch Clayton, Alexandria Bay, Ogdensburg, Prescott, Waddington, Morrisburg, and Louisville, whence stages run to Massena Springs, N. Y. Near Louisville, the steamer enters Long Sault, the first of the celebrated rapids of the St. Lawrence. The descent of these rapids, though not dangerous, is highly exciting, and the tourist will here meet with an experience, such as no other part of the globe will afford. Through these rapids we pass other towns, the old Indian Village of St. Regis, and further on we reach Lachine and the noted Lachine Rapids, the swiftest and most dangerous rapids of the St. Lawrence, around which has been constructed a wide ship canal—a work of stupendous magnitude, and one reflecting great credit upon the enterprise of the citizens of Montreal. Below the Lachine Rapids, we soon reach Montreal, where the tourist should stop a day or two at least, to visit the numerous interesting and beautiful buildings of the metropolis of the Dominion. At Montreal a change is made to the larger and more elegant steamers of the same line that run to Quebec. These steamers almost rival the magnificent floating palaces of the People's and Fall River Lines of New York, and nothing is wanting that can add to the comfort of the traveler as he journeys on to the most interesting and historically famous place of North America—the City of Quebec. From here the route may be continued to the White Mountains, *via* Gorham, N. H., or *via* Lake Memphremagog, or *via* Portland to Boston, or by returning to Montreal, and thence south to New York or Boston. Having once taken this trip the tourist will have been impressed with its marvelous beauty and variety, with the sublime grandeur of the great Lake of Ontario, the charmingly picturesque scenery of the Thousand Islands that stud the emerald waters of the St. Lawrence for fifty miles, the exciting adventure of "Shooting the Rapids," and the interesting, historic cities of Montreal and Quebec—what more could one ask to render the tour of the St. Lawrence eminently delightful ? For a detailed description of the places of interest on this route, we refer the tourist to the "All Round Route Guides," published by Chisholm & Co., of Montreal, and for sale on the steamers.

## CONGRESS HALL, Saratoga Springs, N. Y.

H. S. CLEMENT Manager.     CLEMENT & COX.

Rates:—$3.00, $3.50 and $4.00 per day, according to location of rooms.

## COSMOPOLITAN HOTEL,
### EUROPEAN PLAN,
### Cor. Chambers St. and West Broadway, N. Y.

One of the best hotels in New York for the traveling public. Centrally located and most economical in prices.

*This Hotel has been recently re-fitted and is complete in all its appointments.*

It is centrally located, the principal City Railways pass the door, is five minutes' walk of the New Jersey Central, Pennsylvania, Delaware, Lackawanna and Western, Erie Rail-Roads, all Hudson River Steamboats; within fifteen minutes' ride of Grand Central Depot and Central Park by Elevated Railroad. An Otis Brothers' E'evator carries guests to every floor, rendering all rooms easy of access. The house contains a Barber's Shop with range of Baths, a Railroad Ticket Office where Tickets may be obtained at the same prices as at the depots, a Billiard Room, and a News Office for the sale of Daily and Weekly Papers, Periodicals, Etc.

### "PRICES REDUCED."

Rooms 50 cents, $1.00 per day and upwards. Rooms for two, $1.50 per day and upwards, according to size and location. Family rooms at reduced rates.

**N. & S. J. HUGGINS, Proprietors.**

**First-Class RESTAURANT, at Popular Prices.**

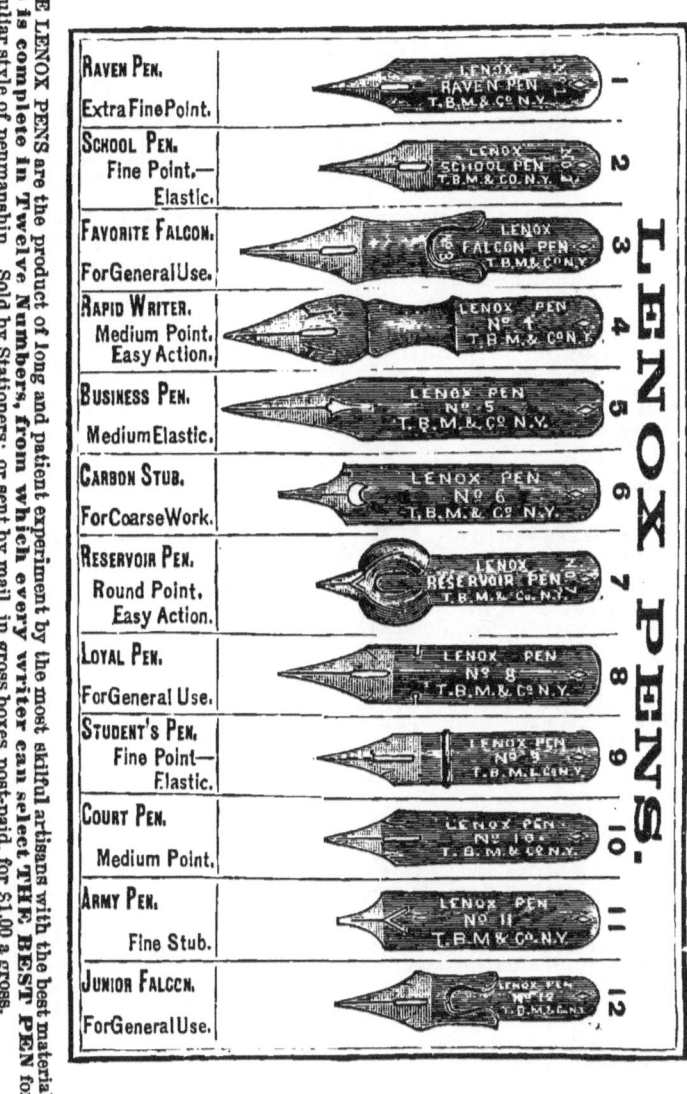

THE LENOX PENS are the product of long and patient experiment by the most skilful artisans with the best material. The Series is complete in Twelve Numbers, from which every writer can select THE BEST PEN for his or her peculiar style of penmanship. Sold by Stationers; or sent by mail, in gross boxes, post-paid, for $1.00 a gross.

\*\*\* For the convenience of those who wish to test all the numbers of the series we will send gross boxes of assorted pens, containing twelve of each number, for the regular gross price of $1.00, one of each number (12 pens) for 10 cents, or two of each kind (24 pens) in a handsome nickle-plated case with spring cover for 25 cents.

**TAINTOR, BROTHERS, MERRILL & CO., 18 and 20 Astor Place, New York City.**

## THE NEW BOOK OF WORSHIP.

# SONGS OF CHRISTIAN PRAISE,
### FOR CHOIR AND CONGREGATION.
#### Published with or without Scripture Selections for Responsive Reading.
##### EDITED BY REV. CHARLES H. RICHARDS, D.D

**SONGS OF CHRISTIAN PRAISE** has already been adopted by many churches throughout the country, and has been received with unqualified satisfaction.

### Testimonials from the Press.

**The New York Observer** says: "It contains everything essential to a handbook for general worship and special services. While it is attractively published, it is furnished at a price which is intended to make it popular."

**The Interior,** Chicago, Ill : " Not burdened with lumber, it is yet large enough for all uses; choice enough to satisfy the most cultivated taste, and popular enough to lead the congregation."

**The Congregationalist,** Boston, Mass.: "It has been compiled with a discriminating wisdom and taste, and edited with a thoroughness which are uncommon."

**The Advance** says: "One of the choicest, richest, and most usable hymn-books published."

**The Golden Rule,** Boston, Mass.: "In its musical part this service-book is probably not surpassed by any other in the language."

**The New York Times:** "In its mechanical arrangement the book leaves scarcely anything to be desired."

### Testimonials from the Pulpit.

**Rev. G. L. Spining, D.D.,** Cleveland, Ohio: "It is the best I have ever seen."

**Rev. C. L. Thompson, D.D.,** Pastor of Presbyterian Church, Kansas City, Mo.: "It is every way an admirable book, convenient in size and shape, rich in hymns and tunes, and fully adapted to all the demands of social and public worship."

**Rev. W. E. Knox, D.D.,** Pastor First Presbyterian Church, Elmira, N. Y.: " Your volume of Christian Praise is very attractive. Mechanically and typographically it is the highest style of art. The hymns I like for their devotional character."

**Rev. J. E. Rankin, D.D.,** Washington, D.C.: "The book is a grand one. Certainly the best of its kind I have ever examined."

**Rev. J. Hall McIlvaine,** Providence, R.I.: "After two years use, I regard ' Songs of Christian Praise' as beyond comparison with any book that I have ever seen."

**Rev. J. G. Vose, D.D.,** Providence, R.I., says: " Our people are unanimous in its favor, and enjoy it more and more."

**Rev. T. M. Monroe,** of Akron, Ohio, says : "The book grows upon us, and we heartily commend it."

**Rev. W. H. Thomas,** says: "Your hymn-book has more than met our expectations. It is a work of merit, and improves with use. It gives perfect satisfaction."

**Rev. Frank P. Woodbury, D.D.,** Rockford, Ill., says : " Our high expectations of the popular acceptance of the book, when, after thorough examination and extensive comparison, we ordered 450 copies, have been more than fulfilled."

**Rev. Samuel Conn, D.D.,** St. Paul, Minn., says : "We decided upon 'Songs of Christian Praise,' after a thorough comparison with several other books. A short trial in actual worship has confirmed our favorable opinion of it."

**Rev. L. O. Brastow, D.D.,** Burlington, Vt., says: "To me personally it is exceedingly satisfactory. It gives satisfaction to the church and congregation."

**Rev. Eli Corwin D.D.,** Racine, Wis., says: "The book is admirable for church service, and is the best for that purpose with which I am acquainted."

Returnable Copies sent free to Pastors or Church Committees desiring books for examination.

A *twenty-four page pamphlet, containing specimen pages, testimonials, price lists, etc., mailed free to any address on application to*

### TAINTOR BROTHERS, MERRILL & CO., Publishers,
#### 18 and 20 Astor Place, New York City.

COMMONWEALTH AVENUE, Showing the Brattle-square Church and the Vendome.

**WASHINGTON, D. C.**

T. E. ROESSLE, - - - Proprietor.

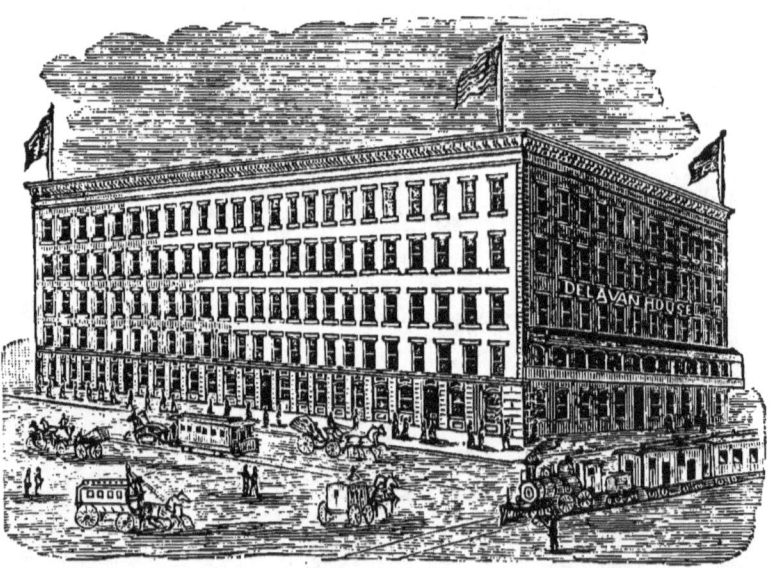

**DELAVAN HOUSE, Albany, N. Y.,**

T. E. ROESSLE & SON, Proprietors.

# FORT WILLIAM HENRY HOTEL.

Opens June 1st. Board for the season, $15, $17.50, $21, $25 and $28 per week, according to the location of rooms.

**T. E. ROESSLE, Proprietor, Lake George, N. Y.**

Also proprietor of the "The Arlington," Washington, D. C., and the Delavan House, Albany, N. Y.

# TAINTOR'S GUIDE-BOOKS

## TAINTOR BROTHERS, MERRILL & CO., Publishers,
### 18 & 20 Astor Place, New York.

These Guides describe all Cities, Towns and Stations on the routes, giving items of interest to the traveler for business and pleasure, and are

### ILLUSTRATED WITH MAPS AND WOODCUTS.

### PRICE, 25 CENTS EACH, BY MAIL.

"**City of New York.**"—Containing descriptions of and directions for visiting the Public Buildings, Places of Amusement, Library, etc. A new Street Directory, Travelers' Directory, and a Map of New York, Brooklyn, Jersey City, Hoboken, etc.

"**Hudson River Route.**"—New York to West Point, Catskill Mountains, Albany, Troy, Saratoga Springs, Lake George, Lake Champlain, Adirondacks, Montreal and Quebec, via Hudson River Steamers.

"**Saratoga Illustrated.**"—The Visitors' Guide to Saratoga Springs, with maps and wood cuts.

"**Saratoga Mineral Waters.**"—Directions for their use by Dr. W. O. Stillman, of Saratoga Springs, N. Y.

**Sea-Side Resorts.**—A Hand-book for Health and Pleasure Seekers, for the Atlantic Coast from the St. Lawrence to the Mississippi.

"**The Northern Resorts.**"—Boston to the White Mountains, Lake Memphremagog, Green Mountains, Lake Champlain, Sheldon, Massena, Ogdensburgh, Montreal and Quebec.

"**The Pennsylvania Coal Regions.**"—New York and Philadelphia to Easton, Bethlehem, Delaware Water Gap, Mauch Chunk, Scranton, Harrisburg, Williamsport and Elmira.

"**The Erie Route.**"—New York to Ithaca, Watkins' Glen, Rochester, Dunkirk, Buffalo and Niagara Falls, via Erie Railway and branches.

"**New York to Saratoga, Buffalo and Niagara Falls.**"—Via Hudson River and New York Central R.R.

"**The Newport and Fall River Route.**" New York to Boston, via Newport and Fall River. With descriptions of Newport and Narragansett Bay.

"**Connecticut River Route.**"—New York to the White Mountains, via N. Y. & N. H. and Connecticut River R.R.

"**New York to Philadelphia, Baltimore and Washington.**"

### Published by TAINTOR BROTHERS, MERRILL & CO.,
### 18 & 20 Astor Place, New York.

# THE NEW YORK HOTEL.

THIS LONG-ESTABLISHED FAVORITE HOTEL HAS BEEN PUT IN COMPLETE ORDER, AND WILL COMPARE FAVORABLY IN ALL RESPECTS WITH ANY FIRST-CLASS HOTEL IN THE UNITED STATES.

SITUATED ON BROADWAY, BETWEEN WASHINGTON AND WAVERLEY PLACES, OCCUPYING THE ENTIRE BLOCK AND A LARGE HOUSE ON BLOCK ADJOINING, CONNECTED BY A BRIDGE. CAPACITY, FIVE HUNDRED GUESTS. A FIRST-CLASS RESTAURANT HAS RECENTLY BEEN OPENED TO ACCOMMODATE GUESTS AND THE PUBLIC GENERALLY.

THE LOCATION IS UNSURPASSED FOR HEALTHFULNESS AND CONVENIENCE OF ACCESS BY SURFACE AND ELEVATED RAILWAYS TO ALL PARTS OF THE CITY.

CONDUCTED ON BOTH AMERICAN AND EUROPEAN PLANS. PRICE OF ROOMS, WITH BOARD, THREE DOLLARS PER DAY; WITHOUT BOARD, ONE DOLLAR AND UPWARD.

H. CRANSTON, Proprietor.

## CRANSTON'S WEST POINT HOTEL,

ON HUDSON—IN THE HIGHLANDS.

H. CRANSTON, - - - Proprietor.

Open from May 1 to November 1.

"*Nature and art have combined to make West Point one of the most picturesque and attractive spots on the continent.*

"*It does not seem possible for one to inhale the pure air of the Highlands, and enjoy the comforts provided by Mr. Cranston, without being made sensible of having received in many respects more or less benefit.*

"*The complete appointments of the house, the high moral tone and standing of the guests, all serve to make a summer spent at Cranston's West Point Hotel one of the most enjoyable ever passed.*"—AUTHOR OF "HUDSON HIGHLANDS."

## MASSASOIT HOUSE,

W. H. CHAPIN,                                                     SPRINGFIELD, MASS.

The Massasoit House, near Railroad Stations, was established in 1843. It has been twice enlarged, making it three times its original size, and thoroughly remodeled and refurnished. The large airy sleeping rooms, furnished with hot and cold water, are excelled by none in the country. Connecting rooms, *en suite*, for families, elegantly furnished and with bath-rooms attached. Special attention paid to ventilation and all sanitary improvements. The proprietors are determined that the world-wide reputation of the Massasoit shall be maintained in all respects.

Perfectly Pure Extracts of Choicest Fruits, THE BEST. Unequaled Strength for all. Thousands of gross sold. Winning friends everywhere. DEALERS TREBLE SALES WITH THEM.

These **Delicious Flavors** are used at many of the **Finest Hotels** in the **White Mountains**, **Saratoga Springs**, the **Catskills**, **Seaside** and **Summer Resorts**, and in **City** and **Country**, and sold by Dealers **Everywhere**. Wholesale Agents in large cities.

LABORATORY (Home Dept.), WESTFIELD, MASS.

# THE CALIGRAPH
## WRITING MACHINE.

### IT STANDS AT THE HEAD.

**15,000 CALIGRAPHS** are in daily use, and are becoming immensely popular for their **Durability, Speed,** and **Manifolding** ability.
We publish 400 letters from prominent men and firms which are convincing.
For specimens, etc., address,

### THE AMERICAN WRITING MACHINE CO.,
### HARTFORD, CONN.
**NEW YORK OFFICE, No. 237 BROADWAY.**

---

# THE CRITIC.

### A WEEKLY REVIEW OF LITERATURE AND THE ARTS.
#### TEN CENTS A COPY; $3 A YEAR.

**Bishop Potter Always Reads "The Critic."**

I am glad of this opportunity to express to you my keen sense of indebtedness for THE CRITIC. I never read it—and, no matter how much driven, I never allow it to go unread—without a fresh conviction of its rare worth. It is so thoroughly just, so discriminating, so full of the atmosphere of a courageous, candid and open-minded criticism, that one cannot but be proud and glad that so good and helpful a journal is winning its way to the wider recognition and esteem which it so abundantly deserves.
H. C. POTTER.

For one who desires a current report from the active world of letters, a knowledge of the best books in every department of Science, Literature and Art, careful critiques upon the principal books by specialists in the several departments of learning—there is no guide so full, scholarly, and satisfactory as THE CRITIC.
New York City. J. H. VINCENT, D. D., *Chancellor Chautauqua University*.

"Undeniably the best literary review in the United States."—*Boston Globe.*

**THE CRITIC COMPANY, 743 Broadway, New York.**

**67th ANNUAL STATEMENT, December 31st, 1886.**

# ÆTNA INSURANCE COMPANY,
## HARTFORD, CONN.

| | |
|---|---:|
| CASH CAPITAL | $4,000,000 00 |
| Reserved for Re-Insurance (Fire) | 1,797,495 06 |
| "          "           (Inland) | 10,692 15 |
| "  Unpaid Losses (Fire) | 206,153 50 |
| "          "      (Inland) | 44,844 82 |
| All other claims | 59,432 66 |
| NET SURPLUS | 3,450,221 37 |
| TOTAL ASSETS | $9,568,839 56 |

### "AS FOLLOWS:"

| | |
|---|---:|
| Cash in Bank | $936,516 64 |
| Cash in hands of Agents | 374,380 20 |
| Real Estate | 358,336 70 |
| Loans on Bond and Mortgage | 43,595 00 |
| Loans on Collaterals | 11,180 00 |
| Stocks and Bonds | 7,843,486 00 |
| Accrued Interest | 1,345 02 |
| TOTAL ASSETS | $9,568,839 56 |

**LOSSES PAID IN 68 YEARS, $60,180,000.**

WM. B. CLARK, Ass't Sec.   J. GOODNOW, Sec.   L. J. HENDEE, Pres't.
JAS. A. ALEXANDER, Agt., 68 Wall St., New York.

---

# ÆTNA LIFE INSURANCE CO.
## OF HARTFORD, CONN.

ASSETS, - - - - - $31,545,930.77

SURPLUS, { by Massachusetts and Conn. Standard, 5,349,870.36
{ by New York Standard, 6,800,000.00

### CONSERVATIVE, ECONOMICAL and "SOLID AS GRANITE."

**POLICIES NON-FORFEITING AND INCONTESTABLE**
after the death of the insured.

All desirable plans of Insurance, including some which are new and especially advantageous.

**ADDRESS THE COMPANY OR ANY OF ITS AGENTS.**

## M. G. BULKELEY, President.

J. C. WEBSTER, Vice-President.          J. L. ENGLISH, Secretary.

# CONNECTICUT
## FIRE INSURANCE COMPANY,
### OF HARTFORD, Conn.

Incorporated 1850.                Charter Perpetual.

| | |
|---|---|
| CASH CAPITAL, | $1,000,000.00 |
| CASH ASSETS, | 2,129,741.94 |

WESTERN DEPARTMENT:
A. WILLIAMS, Manager,
155 La Salle Street,
CHICAGO, Ill.

PACIFIC DEPARTMENT:
ROBERT DICKSON, Manager.
WM. MACDONALD,
Assistant Manager.
SAN FRANCISCO, Cal.

SCOTT & TALBOT, Agents,
45 William St., New York.

J. D. BROWNE, President,    CHAS. R. BURT, Secretary,
L. W. CLARKE, Assistant-Secretary.

# CONGRESS SPRING.
## The Standard Mineral Water.

It is a purely Natural Water, CATHARTIC ALTERATIVE, and slightly stimulating and tonic in its effects, without producing the debility that usually attends a course of medicine.

It is used with marked success in affections of the Liver and Kidneys, and for Dyspepsia, Gout, Constipation and Cutaneous Diseases it is unrivaled.

It is especially beneficial as a general preservative of the tone of the stomach and purity of the blood, and a powerful preventive of Fevers and Bilious Complaints.

It is of special value to Ladies, as from its great purifying properties it has good effect in clearing the skin and giving it a healthy, beautiful appearance. In the morning it tones the appetite and promotes digestion. The stomach is cleansed and purified, the nervous and muscular system invigorated, and germs of disease thrown off.

The superior excellence of Congress Water is evidenced in the *happy proportion* of its several ingredients, which combine to make it so efficient, and in the *absolute solution* in which these pure ingredients are *held* when BOTTLED, making it, without doubt, one of the best and *safest saline cathartic waters* ever discovered either in this country or Europe.

As a cathartic water its almost entire freedom from *iron* should recommend it above all others, many of which contain so much of this ingredient as to seriously impair their usefulness.

### CAUTIONARY SIGNAL.

All mineral waters **strongly impregnated** with **iron**, when drank with freedom (especially when fasting), while injurious to all, are to persons of certain constitution and temperament **positively dangerous,** owing to the powerful action of the **iron** in combination with the carbonic acid gas, which tends to accelerate the action of the **heart** and cause **powerful pressure** on the **brain;** thereby producing those results that so often **fatally** follow the cause.

The above **caution** is necessary, the real amount of **iron** not being fully put forth in the **analysis** of several mineral spring waters.

☞ For sale (in Bottles only) by all leading Druggists, Grocers, Wine Merchants and Hotels. Address,

## CONGRESS SPRING CO.,
### SARATOGA SPRINGS, N. Y.

## HUDSON RIVER BY DAYLIGHT.

# DAY LINE STEAMERS,

### "NEW YORK" AND "ALBANY,"

Leave New York, Vestry St., Pier 39, N. R. (adjoining Jersey City Ferry), 8.40 A. M., and foot 22d St., N. R., 9 A. M., landing at Yonkers, West Point, Newburgh, Poughkeepsie, Rhinebeck, Catskill and Hudson. Returning, leave Albany, 8.30 A. M., from foot of Hamilton St., arriving in New York at 5.30 P. M.

## CHOICE OF TWO ROUTES
### TO THE
# RESORTS OF THE CATSKILLS.

### CONNECTIONS.

*BROOKLYN*—Annex leaves Fulton Street at 8.00 A. M. Leaves Vestry Street Pier on arrival of down boat.

*WEST POINT*—With Stages for **Cranston's** and **West Point Hotels**, and with down boat at 2.50.

*NEWBURGH*—With down boat at 2.15.

*RHINEBECK*—With Ferry for **Rondout**, and Ulster & Delaware R. R. for *Catskill Mountain Resorts*, and Wallkill Valley R. R. for **Lake Mohonk**.

*CATSKILL*—With Catskill Mountain R. R.

*HUDSON*—With Boston and Albany R. R., for Chatham, Pittsfield, North Adams, Lebanon Springs, etc.

*ALBANY*—With through trains for Utica, Alexandria Bay, Geneva, **Niagara Falls, Buffalo, Watertown, Thousand Islands** and Western Points. Special trains to and from **Saratoga**. Through tickets sold to all points.

### DINING SALOON ON THE MAIN DECK.
*Meals served on the European Plan.*
### MUSIC THROUGHOUT THE TRIP.

☞ TRIP TICKETS from New York to West Point or Newburgh returning same day.

1794. 1887.

# HARTFORD
# Fire Insurance Co.

### OF HARTFORD, CONN.

*STATEMENT JANUARY 1, 1887.*

| | |
|---|---:|
| Cash Capital, | $1,250,000 00 |
| Reserve for Re-Insurance (legal standard), | 1,764,932 23 |
| Outstanding Claims, | 251,027 48 |
| Policy Holders' Surplus, | 3,039,986 74 |
| Net Surplus over Capital and All Liabilities, | 1,789,986 74 |
| **Total Assets,** | **$5,055,946 45** |
| Net Premiums received during the year, | $2,350,371 59 |
| Total Income received during the year, | 2,561,066 97 |
| Increase in Assets, | 310,604 53 |
| Increase in Net Surplus, | 346,627 53 |

GEO. L. CHASE, *President.*

P. C. ROYCE, *Secretary.*     THOMAS-TURNBULL, *Ass't Secretary.*

## WESTERN DEPARTMENT.

G. F. BISSELL,                             *General Agent.*
P. P. HEYWOOD,                 *Assistant General Agent.*

**CHICAGO, ILL.**

## PACIFIC DEPARTMENT.

BELDEN & COFRON,                     *Managers.*

**SAN FRANCISCO, CAL.**

## BRANCH OFFICE.

**158 BROADWAY,**                   **NEW YORK.**

GEORGE M. COIT, *Agent.*

MAKES A SPECIALTY OF

# SUMMER RESORT NEWS.

The Paper will be sent to any address for

## 75 CENTS A MONTH.

---

The Tribune is delivered every Sunday at nearly all the Northern Summer Resorts by

### SPECIAL FAST TRAIN,

Run solely to carry Newspapers.

---

## THE TRIBUNE LEADS

all the New York papers in enterprise and interest, and

**DOES NOT DEPEND ON**

SENSATION AND TRASH FOR CIRCULATION.

---

75 Cents a Month, or $8.50 a Year.

# TOURISTS' IDEAL ROUTE,
## NIAGARA TO THE SEA.
# ROME, WATERTOWN & OGDENSBURG R. R.

Great Highway and Favorite Route for Fashionable Pleasure Travel.
Only All-Rail Route to Thousand Islands.

1887.　　NEW FAST TRAINS, AVOIDING STOPS.　　1887.

## WAGNER PALACE SLEEPING CARS.

**NEW YORK AND PAUL SMITH'S, 15 Hours.**
**NEW YORK AND CLAYTON, 11 Hours.**
**NIAGARA FALLS AND CLAYTON, 9½ Hours.**
**NIAGARA FALLS AND PORTLAND, MAINE, 24 Hours.**

Via Norwood, Fabyans, Crawford Notch, and all White Mountain Resorts.

## WAGNER PALACE DRAWING-ROOM CARS.

NIAGARA FALLS AND CLAYTON.
ROCHESTER AND CLAYTON.
SYRACUSE AND CLAYTON.
ALBANY AND CLAYTON.
UTICA AND CLAYTON.

Direct and immediate connections are made at Clayton with powerful steamers for Alexandria Bay and all Thousand Island Resorts, also with Rich. & Ont. Nav. Co. Steamers for Montreal, Quebec and River Saguenay, passing all of the Thousand Islands and Rapids of the River St. Lawrence by daylight. For tickets, time-tables and further information apply to nearest ticket agent or correspond with General Passenger Agent, Oswego, N. Y.

### ROUTES AND RATES FOR SUMMER TOURS.

A beautiful book of 150 pages, profusely illustrated, contains maps, cost of tours, list of hotels, and describes over 300 Combination Summer Tours via Thousand Islands and Rapids of the St. Lawrence River, Saguenay River, Gulf of St. Lawrence, Lake Champlain, Lake George, White Mountains, to Portland, Kennebunk, Boston, New York and all Mountain, Lake, River and Sea Shore Resorts in Canada, New York and New England. It is the best book given away. Send ten cents postage to General Passenger Agent, Oswego, N. Y., for a copy before deciding upon your summer trip.

THEO. BUTTERFIELD,
H. M. BRITTON,　　　　Gen'l Passenger Agent,
Gen'l Manager.　　　　　OSWEGO, N. Y.

# Saratoga Kissingen Spring

## Natural Mineral Water.

Unsurpassed as an aperient, diuretic and alterative. Highly effervescent, and unexcelled as a TABLE WATER.

Very efficacious in its action upon the stomach, liver and kidneys, and is a great aid to digestion.

### THE SARATOGA KISSINGEN

has more fixed gas than any other Natural Mineral Spring Water in this country. It is, therefore, the most marketable, as it retains all its qualities after bottling, and without regard to climate.

---

### DIRECTIONS.

**As an Aperient**—Drink before breakfast one pint, at a moderate temperature.

**As a Diuretic**—Take in smaller quantities frequently during the day.

**For Indigestion**—Take one glassful just before or after meals.

---

For sale in cases of four dozen pints, or two dozen quarts, and to the trade, for draught purposes, in block-tin-lined barrels.

All orders should be addressed to

### SARATOGA KISSINGEN COMPANY,
Saratoga Springs, N. Y.

Or, No. 11 West 27th Street, New York City.

SARATOGA OFFICE,
No. 3 GRAND UNION BLOCK.

# PEOPLE'S EVENING LINE
### BETWEEN
## NEW YORK AND ALBANY.

During the Season of Navigation, the Steamers

## DREW or DEAN RICHMOND,

*Capt. S. J. ROE.*        *Capt. THOS. POST,*

**WILL LEAVE NEW YORK FOR ALBANY,**

Daily, Sundays excepted, at 6 P. M., from Pier 41 (Old No.) North River, Foot of Canal Street.

Connecting with trains for SARATOGA, LAKE GEORGE, LAKE CHAMPLAIN, the ADIRONDACKS and Summer Resorts of the NORTH, EAST AND WEST.

### Saratoga Office, 369 Broadway.

**LEAVE ALBANY.**

Every week-day at 8 P. M., or on arrival of trains from NORTH, EAST and WEST, connecting at New York with ALL EARLY TRAINS for the SOUTH. Meals on the European Plan.

### FOR TICKETS IN NEW YORK

Apply at Company's Office (Pier 41 North River); and at all principal Hotels and Ticket Offices in New York, and on board the Steamers. R. R. Office throughout the country.

 Tickets sold and baggage checked to all points WEST via N. Y. C. & H. R R., N. Y. & W. S., D. & H. C. Co., Fitchburg, Cent'l Vt., B. & A., and O. & L. C. Railroads, etc.

W. W. EVERETT,    J. H. ALLAIRE,    M. B. WATERS,
  *President.*     *Gen'l T. Agent.*    *Gen Pass Agent.*

# WILLARD'S HOTEL,

## WASHINGTON, D. C.

---

This old-established and chosen rendezvous and favorite abiding-place of the most famous men and women of America has, under the present management, been thoroughly renovated at an expense of over $100,000, and is now pronounced as the model Hotel in regard to luxurious apartments, cuisine, service and system for heating and ventilation.

The "WILLARD" is located within a stone's-throw of the Executive Mansion, Treasury, War, Navy and State Departments, the Department of Justice, Corcoran Art Gallery, and other numerous points of interest, and can justly be called the most convenient Hotel for tourists and other travelers in Washington City.

O. G. STAPLES, Proprietor.

Formerly of the Thousand Island House.

DRINK THE GENUINE
# EXCELSIOR WATER
## OF SARATOGA.

**CURES DYSPEPSIA, HEADACHES, CONSTIPATION, ETC.**

Sold on Draught and in Bottles by First-class Druggists and Hotels.

TRADE MARK.

The Genuine **EXCELSIOR WATER** is sold on Draught only through the Trade Mark. Ask your druggist for it, and be sure you get the "**EXCELSIOR**" drawn through the Trade Mark as shown in the annexed sketch. Avoid Artificial and Recharged Waters.

The "Excelsior" Water is unequalled as a cathartic and diuretic, and is used with great success in treating diseases of the Liver and Kidneys. See below letters from two of our best known medical men.

*From Fordyce Barker, M. D., of New York.*

I make great use of the various mineral waters in my practice, and I regard the "Excelsior" Spring Water of Saratoga as the best saline and alkaline laxative of this class. Sparkling with Carbonic Acid Gas, it is to most persons very agreeable to the taste, and prompt in action as a gentle Diuretic and Cathartic.

FORDYCE BARKER, M. D.

*From Alfred L. Loomis, M. D., of New York.*

During my whole professional life I have been accustomed to use freely the Water of Congress and Empire Springs. About six months since, accidentally, I was furnished with a few bottles of the "Excelsior" Spring Water, and found it so much more agreeable to the taste and pleasant in its effects than either Congress or Empire Water, that I have since used it myself, and recommend it to patients requiring a gentle Cathartic and Diuretic. A. L. LOOMIS, M. D.

THE BOTTLED "EXCELSIOR" WATER is unexcelled, and retains all its properties unimpaired for years.

Address FRANK W. LAWRENCE,
**Proprietor Excelsior and Union Springs,**
SARATOGA SPRINGS, N. Y.

## DRS. STRONG'S REMEDIAL INSTITUTE,
*Saratoga Springs, N. Y.*

POPULAR SUMMER RESORT. **Open all the year.** Receives patients or boarders, permanent or transient. Location central, quiet, shady and within three minutes' walk of the large hotels, principal springs, Congress Park, and other sources of attraction. Fine Lawn Tennis and Croquet Grounds. Desirable rooms, extensive piazzas, ample grounds. **Table and appointments First-Class.** Heated by steam. The bath department is complete and elegant, affording **Turkish, Russian, Roman and Electro-thermal Baths.**

Genial, cultured society and a pleasant home are always found here. It is the resort of many eminent persons for rest and recreation Among its patrons and references are Rev. THEO. L. CUYLER, D D. (Brooklyn); Rev. CHAS. F. DEEMS, D. D. (N. Y); Rev. R. D. HARPER, D. D. (Philadelphia); Rev. C. C. "Chaplain" McCABE (Chicago); Rev. Dr. JNO. POTTS (Ottawa); Bishops FOSS and HARRIS; Hon. F. C. SESSIONS (Columbus, O.); J. M. PHILLIPS (M. E. Book Concern, N. Y.); JAS. MCCREERY (N. Y.); Ex-Gov. WELLS (Va.); Presidents MCCOSH (Princeton), HITCHCOCK (Union Theol. Sem.), WARREN (Boston Univ.); Judges REYNOLDS (Brooklyn), DRAKE (Washington), HAND (Penn). BLISS (Mo.); Med. Profs. Ross (Chicago), KNAPP, (N. Y.), FORD (Ann Arbor), and many others equally known.

During the entire year the Institute is made specially attractive to its guests by frequent entertainments of varied character. There is no appearance of invalidism. The remedial and hotel interests in no way interfere, patients receiving at all times every care and attention. The proprietors are "regular" physicians, graduates of the Medical Department, University of the City of New York. The Institute is the largest and best in Saratoga, and one of the most complete in its appointments in the country, and is endorsed and largely patronized by the medical profession. Besides the ordinary remedial agents available in general practice, such special appliances are used as Massage, Turkish, Russian, Roman, Electro-thermal, Hydropathic Baths; Galvanic and Faradic Electricity, Pneumatic Cabinet, Vacuum Treatment, Movement Cure, Compressed Air, Oxygen and Medicated Inhalations, Health Lift, Calisthenics, and the Mineral Waters. *SEND FOR CIRCULAR.*

# SARATOGA GEYSER WATER!

"Applicable to a Greater Number of Persons than any other Water at Saratoga."

*FOR DYSPEPSIA* it is unrivalled. It contains more Soda and Magnesia combined than any other Saratoga water.

*FOR KIDNEY DISEASES* it, beyond dispute, excels all other waters. It contains a *much larger quantity of Lithia* than any of the so-called Lithia waters.

*AS A CATHARTIC,* when taken rather warm before breakfast, it is *mild yet thorough.* It is not a harsh water.

### BEWARE OF MANUFACTURED WATER.

### Ask for SARATOGA Geyser.

For Sale by the Glass, fresh from the Bottle, at our office, cor. Broadway and Congress Sts., Saratoga Springs, N. Y.

ADDRESS,

## GEYSER SPRING CO.,
Saratoga Springs, N. Y.

# THE INDEPENDENT.

"One of the ablest weeklies in existence."—*Pall Mall Gazette*, London, England.

"The most influential religious organ in the States."—*The Spectator*, London, England.

"Clearly stands in the fore-front as a weekly religious magazine."—*Sunday-School Times*, Philadelphia.

It is a Newspaper, Magazine and Review all in one. It is a religious, a literary, an educational, a story, an art, a scientific, an agricultural, a financial and a political paper combined. It has thirty-two folio pages and twenty-two departments.

### PROMINENT FEATURES ARE:
*Religious and Theological Articles;*
*Social and Political Articles;*
*Articles of Description and Travel;*
*Weekly Literary Articles;*
*Poems and Stories.*

No one who has ever read a copy of **THE INDEPENDENT** will say that it is second to any other weekly journal,

In the quantity and quality of its contents;
In the variety and interest of its ample pages;
In the volume and character of information it gives;
In the diversity and ability of its corps of writers;
In the purity and vigor of its literary tone;
In the candor and clearness of its opinions; or
In the strength and constancy with which it strikes for all that is true and noble in family, social, national and religious life.

### TERMS TO SUBSCRIBERS.

| | | |
|---|---|---|
| Three Months, - - $0 75 | One Year, - - - $3 00 |
| Four Months, - - - 1 00 | Two Years, - - - 5 00 |
| Six Months, - - - 1 50 | Five Years, - - - 10 00 |

Can anyone make a better investment of $2.00 to $3.00 than one which will pay

### 52 Dividends During the Year?

A good way to make the acquaintance of THE INDEPENDENT is to send 30 cents for a "*Trial Trip*" of a month. SPECIMEN COPIES FREE.

## THE INDEPENDENT,

P. O. Box 2787.            251 Broadway, N. Y.

**WASHINGTON, D. C.**

T. E. ROESSLE, - - Proprietor.

**DELAVAN HOUSE, Albany, N. Y.,**
T. E. ROESSLE & SON, Proprietors.

## FORT WILLIAM HENRY HOTEL.

Opens June 1st. Board for the season, $15, $17.50, $21, $25 and $28 per week, according to the location of rooms.

T. E. ROESSLE, Proprietor, Lake George, N. Y.

Also proprietor of the "The Arlington," Washington, D. C., and the Delavan House Albany, N. Y.

## WM. H. McCULLY,
## DESIGNER and ENGRAVER,
### 318 Broadway, New York.

Views of Buildings, Machinery; Portraits, Newspaper and Advertising Cuts of every description.

ILLUSTRATIONS MADE FROM PHOTOGRAPHS.

All work done in the cheapest, neatest and best possible manner.

---

## TAINTOR'S NEW YORK CITY GUIDE.

**City of New York.**—Containing descriptions of and directions for visiting the Public Buildings, etc., with numerous illustrations. A new Street Directory, Travelers' Directory, and a map of New York. Price 25 cents, by mail.

### Published by TAINTOR BROTHERS & CO.,
18 and 20 Astor Place, New York.

---

# THE DOCTOR

## A UNIQUE PUBLICATION DEVOTED TO PHYSICIANS.

Published on the 1st and 16th of Each Month.

—BY—

## CHARLES AVERY WELLES,

No. 20 Astor Place,        New York City.

**Single Copies, 10c. Subscription Per Year, $2.00.**

It is the gossip companion of the physician, and can be read with understanding, interest and profit by the doctor's unprofessional friends. A series of articles upon the healthfulness of summer resorts is now appearing in THE DOCTOR.

# THE UNEXCELLED

## UNQUESTIONABLY UNEQUALLED.  UNIVERSALLY USED.

The Four Largest, Finest, Most Novel and Best Managed Displays of

# FIREWORKS

EVER PRODUCED WERE THOSE AT

The Centennial at Newburgh, N. Y., October 18, 1883.
The Presidential Inauguration at Washington, D. C., March 4, 1885.
The Bi-Centennial at Albany, N. Y., July 22, 1886, and
The Unveiling of the Bartholdi Statue of Liberty, at the City of New York, on November 1, 1886.

THEY WERE MANUFACTURED AND FIRED BY

## THE UNEXCELLED FIREWORKS CO.,
(INCORPORATED 1874.)

### 9 and 11 Park Place, New York.

Largest Manufacturers.   Only Importers.   Leading and Most Reliable House in

**FIREWORKS, FLAGS, LANTERNS, BALLOONS and DECORATION GOODS.**

Western House, 519 Locust Street, St. Louis, Mo.

Send for Illustrated Catalogue—FREE.

Most Delicious of Saratoga Waters.

IT CORRECTS ACIDITY OF THE STOMACH, ASSISTS DIGESTION AND REGULATES THE KIDNEYS.

## A FINE TABLE WATER,

It Mixes Well with Syrup, Wines or Milk.

## BEWARE OF ARTIFICIAL VICHYS!

THE SARATOGA VICHY is a Pure, Natural Water; all other Vichy drawn from fountains is manufactured. Ask your Druggist or Grocer for the SARATOGA VICHY, or address,

## SARATOGA VICHY SPRING CO.,

Saratoga Springs, N. Y.

**W. D. GARRISON, Manager.**

600 handsomely furnished rooms at $1.00 per day and upwards. European Plan.

First-class Restaurant, Dining Rooms, Café and Lunch Counter *a la carte*, at moderate prices.

Guests' Baggage to and from Grand Central Depot free. Carriage Hire saved.

Travelers can live well at the Grand Union for less money than at any other first-class hotel in New York.

# THE NEW YORK OBSERVER.

## The Oldest and Best Family Paper in the World.

### IT HAS ALL THE NEWS:

### FOREIGN AND DOMESTIC LETTERS:

**LITERARY, BUSINESS, AGRICULTURAL, HOUSEHOLD, CHILDREN'S AND TEACHERS' DEPARTMENTS.**

Vigorous treatment of current topics;
Opinions worth having;
There is no other paper like it.
Send for a sample copy free.

*ADVERTISERS FIND IT A SURE MEDIUM TO REACH CUSTOMERS.*

Address **NEW YORK OBSERVER**, NEW YORK.

# C. W. MOULTON & CO.'S PUBLICATIONS.

# QUERIES

A MONTHLY REVIEW OF LITERARY ART, SCIENTIFIC AND GENERAL EDUCATIONAL QUESTIONS OF THE DAY.

ILLUSTRATED.

One Dollar Per Annum. Single Copies Ten Cents.

## QUERIES WITH ANSWERS.
### FIRST SERIES.

Two thousand, eight hundred twenty-five Questions with Answers on American History, The Antiquary, Art, Astronomy, Chemistry, Classical Mythology, Commerce and Manufacture, The Drama, Education, English Grammar, History of France, General History, Geography, German Literature, American Literature, English Literature, Literature of Greece, General Literature, Mathematics, Maxims, Medicine, Modern Europe, Music, Natural History, Problems, Questions of the Day, Science, Theology, United States History and many other miscellaneous subjects.

**Neatly bound in cloth with stamp on side, 8vo.
Price One Dollar, post paid.**

## QUERIES WITH ANSWERS.
### SECOND SERIES.

Over three thousand Questions prepared by prominent Educators on Chemistry, Military History, Pilgrims and Shrines, Finance, Journalism, German Literature, Agriculture, Biology, Study of Words, History of France, Literature of Greece, Facetious Geography, History of Rome, Facetious Literature, Ecclesiastical History, Geology and Paleontology, History of New York, Philology, Botany, Syntax, Roman Literature, Shakespeariana, History of Philosophy, History of Kansas, Physics, etc., etc.

**12mo Cloth. Price One Dollar, post paid.**

## PRIZE SELECTIONS.

BEING FAMILIAR QUOTATIONS FROM ENGLISH AND AMERICAN POETS, FROM CHAUCER TO THE PRESENT TIME.
Selected and arranged by C. W. MOULTON, Editor of "*Queries.*"

The work consists of eight hundred and twenty-five familiar quotations selected from prominent English and American Poets. 16mo, cloth, pp. 242. $1.00. Three Hundred Dollars in Cash Prizes will be awarded by the publishers to the persons who will name the author of the greatest number of Prize Selections. Competition open until March 15, 1888. Nineteen prizes will be declared. Every purchaser of the book is entitled to compete. For further particulars obtain a copy of the work. Descriptive circular free.

### C. W. MOULTON & CO.,
PUBLISHERS AND BOOKSELLERS.
BUFFALO, N. Y.

Also HOTEL POMENAH, Milford Springs, N. H. Post Office and Telegraph address, Amherst Station, N. H., B. & L. R. R., 48 Miles from Boston. Open from July to November.

C. A. GLEASON, Manager.   BARNES & DUNKLEE, Proprietors.

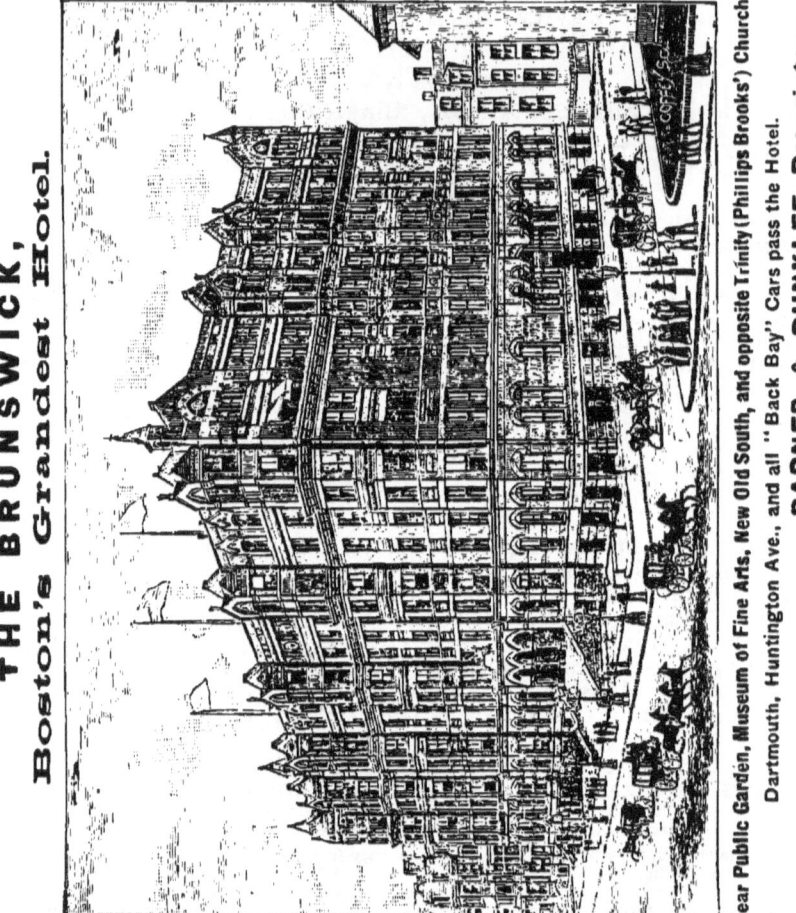

HOTEL POMENAH—Milford Springs, N. H. Post Office and Telegraph address, Amherst Station, N.H., B. & L. R. R. 48 Miles from Boston. Open July to November.

C. A. GLEASON, Manager. BARNES & DUNKLEE, of the Brunswick, Proprietors.

**THE VICTORIA,**
Dartmouth and Newbury Streets, Boston.
**EUROPEAN PLAN.**
In the Centre of the Back Bay District.
BARNES & DUNKLEE, of the Brunswick, Proprietors.
C. A. GLEASON, Manager.

# BOSTON CONGREGATIONALIST.

While the "Congregationalist" stands as the representative of conservative Congregationalism, it is thoroughly awake to the demands of the times, and liberal and progressive in all that is in the interests of religion, morality, and the public welfare generally. It has an editorial representative in New York, and also in Chicago, an ample corps of assistant editors in the home office, and numerous correspondence in different parts of the country, and is thus able to furnish from week to week a great variety of fresh and attractive matter on topics of general interest. It is a family paper, and designed to meet the tastes and needs of different classes, and to promote all that is good and pure and elevating in the family and the church and the community.

The "Congregationalist" stands highest among weekly religious newspapers as an advertising medium, and is the recognized denominational organ. Its circulation is scattered throughout New England and the entire country.

## ADVERTISING,

Twenty-Five Cents per Line, with Discounts.

---

### W. L. GREENE & CO.

COMMONWEALTH AVENUE, Showing the Brattle-square Church and the Hotel Vendome, BOSTON.

# ELY'S CREAM BALM

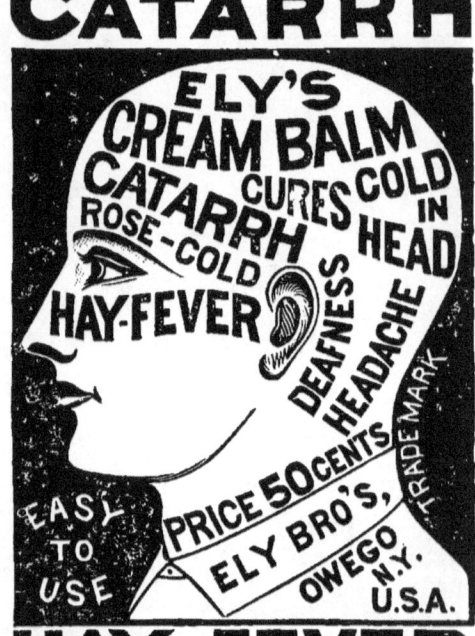

Cleanses the Head.

Allays Inflammation. Heals Sores.

Restores the Senses of Taste, Hearing and Smell.

A Quick Relief.

A Positive Cure.

## UNEQUALED FOR COLDS IN THE HEAD.

I have suffered from acute inflammation in my nose and head. My eye has been for a week at a time so I could not see. I have used no end of remedies, also employed a doctor, who said it was impure blood—but I got no help. I used Ely's Cream Balm on the recommendation of a friend. I was faithless, but in a few days was cured. My nose, now, and also my eye, is well. It is wonderful how quick it helped me. Mrs. GEORGIE S. JUDSON, Hartford, Conn.

I have been a severe sufferer from Catarrh for the past fifteen years, with distressing pain over my eyes. Gradually the disease worked down upon my lungs. About a year and a half ago I commenced using Ely's Cream Balm, with most gratifying results, and am to-day apparently cured. Z. C. WARREN, Rutland, Vt.

## HAY FEVER.

Messrs. ELY BROS., Owego, N. Y.: I have been afflicted for twenty years during the months of August and September with Hay Fever, and have tried various remedies for its relief without success. I was induced to try your Cream Balm; have used it with favorable results, and can confidently recommend it to all similarly afflicted. ROBERT W. TOWNLEY, (Ex-Mayor) Elizabeth, N. J.

CATARRH AND HAY FEVER.—For twenty years I was a sufferer from Catarrh of the head and throat, in a very aggravated form, and during the summer with Hay Fever. I procured a bottle of Ely's Cream Balm, and after a few applications received decided benefit—was cured by one bottle. Have had no return of the complaint. CHARLOTTE PARKER, Waverly, N. Y.

Messrs. WHITE & BURDICK, Druggists, Ithaca, N. Y.: I recommend to those suffering (as I have been) with Hay Fever, Ely's Cream Balm. Have tried nearly all the remedies I could find, and give this a decided preference over them all. It has given me immediate relief. C. T. STEPHENS, Hardware Merchant, Ithaca, N. Y.

www.ingramcontent.com/pod-product-compliance
Lightning Source LLC
Chambersburg PA
CBHW030304170426
43202CB00009B/872